Research Report
November 2011

CONSORTIUM ON CHICAGO SCHOOL RESEARCH AT THE UNIVERSITY OF CHICAGO

Rethinking Teacher Evaluation in Chicago
Lessons Learned from Classroom Observations, Principal-Teacher Conferences, and District Implementation

Authors: Lauren Sartain, Sara Ray Stoelinga, and Eric R. Brown; **with:** Stuart Luppescu, Kavita Kapadia Matsko, Frances K. Miller, Claire E. Durwood, Jennie Y. Jiang, and Danielle Glazer

Acknowledgements

We gratefully acknowledge the Joyce Foundation for its continued support of this critical and timely work, and especially John Luczak for his assistance and thoughtful advice. We thank Chicago Public Schools, especially the Excellence in Teaching Project staff: Sheri Frost Leo, Sheila Cashman, Amy Silverman, Cindy Moyer, and Nicole Cox-Lofton. Without their assistance, this work would not be possible. Also critical to this study is the participation of the pilot principals and teachers—we thank them for generously sharing their time, classrooms and schools, and perspectives with us. Throughout the course of this work, we have convened an advisory group of various stakeholders led by Larry Stanton. This group pushed our thinking and helped to guide the study as it unfolded. We would also like to acknowledge external reviewers who provided feedback on versions of this report, including Audrey Soglin, Larry Stanton, Sheila Cashman, Meghan Zefran, Amy Nowell, Milan Sevak, and Kathleen St. Louis.

Our colleagues at the Consortium on Chicago School Research also read numerous versions of this report and helped to guide the analysis of the data. Marisa de la Torre dug into the nuts and bolts of the classroom observation data and was an important consultant for the reliability and validity analyses. David Stevens provided critical advice regarding the qualitative analyses. A special thanks goes out to Emily Krone, who was an essential thought partner throughout the course of this study and who always pushed for us to communicate succinctly and with purpose. Elaine Allensworth, Sue Sporte, Emily Krone, Paul Goren, David Stevens, and Penny Sebring read the report thoroughly, and their insights and input are reflected here. Sue Sporte also performed a comprehensive technical read of the penultimate draft. Finally, thanks to John Easton of the Institute of Education Sciences for providing the study design and getting this work off the ground. We benefited immensely from John's vision for this project.

For information on this study, contact Lauren Sartain at lsartain@uchicago.edu.

Table of Contents

Executive Summary

In 2008, Chicago Public Schools (CPS) launched the Excellence in Teaching Pilot, an effort to revamp how teachers are evaluated and how they receive feedback on their performance. The pilot was at the forefront of a national movement to redesign teacher evaluation. The work in Chicago and across the country to improve evaluation was motivated by two main factors. First, evaluation systems were failing to give teachers either meaningful feedback on their instructional practices or guidance about what is expected of them in the classroom. Second, traditional teacher evaluation systems were not differentiating among the best teachers, good teachers, and poor teachers. Chicago, for example, relied on a system that both teachers and principals viewed as arbitrary and unfair.[1] Moreover, the system identified 93 percent of teachers as either Superior or Excellent—at the same time that 66 percent of CPS schools were failing to meet state standards, suggesting a major disconnect between classroom results and classroom evaluations.

This report summarizes findings from a two-year study of Chicago's Excellence in Teaching Pilot, which was designed to drive instructional improvement by providing teachers with evidence-based feedback on their strengths and weaknesses. The pilot consisted of training and support for principals and teachers, principal observations of teaching practice conducted twice a year using the Charlotte Danielson Framework for Teaching, and conferences between the principal and the teacher to discuss evaluation results and teaching practice.

Although the findings from this report focus on a specific pilot in a specific city, they have broad implications for districts and states nationwide that are working to design and develop evaluation systems that rely on classroom observations to differentiate among teachers and drive instructional improvement. Overall, we found that the Excellence in Teaching Pilot was an improvement on the old evaluation system and worked as it was designed and intended, introducing an evidence-based observation approach to evaluating teachers and creating a shared definition of effective teaching. At the same time, the new system faced a number of challenges, including weak instructional coaching skills and lack of buy-in among some principals. Specific findings include:

- **The classroom observation ratings were valid measures of teaching practice**; that is, students showed the greatest growth in test scores in the classrooms where teachers received the highest ratings on the Danielson Framework, and students showed the least growth in test scores in classrooms where teachers received the lowest ratings.

- **The classroom observation ratings were reliable measures of teaching practice**; that is, principals and trained observers who watched the same lesson consistently gave the teacher the same ratings; however, 11 percent of principals consistently gave lower ratings than the observers and 17 percent of principals consistently gave higher ratings than the observers.

- **Principals and teachers said that conferences were more reflective and objective than in the past and were focused on instructional practice and improvement.** However, many principals lack the instructional coaching skills required to have deep discussions about teaching practice.

- **Over half of principals were highly engaged in the new evaluation system.** Principals who were not engaged in the new evaluation system tended to say that it was too labor intensive given the numerous district initiatives being simultaneously implemented in their schools.

This report is divided into five chapters:

CHAPTER ONE presents the national impetus for revitalizing teacher evaluation practices and details the teacher evaluation pilot in Chicago and the Charlotte Danielson Framework for Teaching. This chapter provides information that is particularly useful for those interested in how the local and national discussion around teacher evaluation has played out in Chicago, as well as the details of the research behind this report.

CHAPTER TWO investigates the relationship between teacher classroom observation ratings and value-added measures, providing information that might be particularly useful for those working to build an observation system that is linked to learning gains.

CHAPTER THREE describes how principals rated teaching practice across schools when compared to another observer. This chapter provides information for those working to build an observation system where teachers reliably receive the same rating for exhibiting the same quality of instruction.

CHAPTER FOUR highlights the conference component of the evaluation system—principal and teacher reports on the quality of the conversations, as well as an investigation of the nature of these conversations. This chapter provides information for those interested in how a comprehensive evaluation system can be designed to drive instructional improvement.

CHAPTER FIVE follows a different format than the previous chapters and is meant to serve as a design guide for districts and unions that are revitalizing teacher evaluation systems. Instead of providing explicit answers to design questions, the chapter draws attention to key design and logistical considerations and brings evidence from the Chicago pilot to bear on these issues. The goal is to give policymakers and practitioners empirical evidence that they can use to arrive at informed solutions for their own states and districts. Specifically, we discuss criteria for assigning formal evaluation ratings, decisions about classroom observation logistics, training for principals and teachers, principal engagement, and evaluator feedback and accountability. For each of these topics, we provide evidence from the Chicago pilot. We also list some questions for stakeholders to consider when thinking about each of these issues.

Chapter 1

The Context for Revitalizing Teacher Evaluation

Districts and states across the country are engaging in efforts to redesign teacher evaluation systems. Two main factors have motivated this movement. First, teachers generally did not receive meaningful feedback on their instructional practices and had little guidance about what was expected of them in the classroom. Second, traditional teacher evaluation systems did not differentiate among high- and low-performing teachers. In Chicago, for example, historically 93 percent of all of the teachers were in the top two categories of the performance evaluation rating scale while only 0.3 percent were identified as Unsatisfactory.[2] Districts need an evaluation system that accurately captures teacher performance in order to make personnel decisions, such as removing and remediating low-performing teachers or rewarding excellent teachers.

If two primary objectives of evaluations are to provide teachers with information that they can use to improve their teaching practices and to provide teachers with evaluation ratings that accurately capture their classroom performance, then research confirms that traditional evaluation systems are broken. They typically fail to provide teachers with the information they need to make timely and effective improvements in their instructional practice.[3] Often, they rely upon a single observation by a principal, who is minimally trained as an evaluator.[4] At the same time, many evaluation tools are seen as subjective, rendering evaluation meaningless.[5] It is of particular concern that most evaluation systems do not differentiate between strong and weak instruction and therefore fail to identify or facilitate the removal of low-performing teachers.[6]

Policymakers and others have responded to flaws in the current systems by demanding that districts start using data on student academic growth to evaluate teachers. The U.S. Department of Education advanced this agenda by requiring states competing for $4.35 billion in federal Race to the Top funds to remove any existing legal barriers to linking student achievement data to teacher evaluations.[7]

States and districts have responded. In Illinois, lawmakers passed the Performance Evaluation Reform Act of 2010. The legislation requires all districts to implement a standards-based teacher evaluation system with a student achievement indicator, as well as classroom observations using a rubric that outlines best practices. The legislation also specifies a gradual timeline for all districts in Illinois to adopt this approach to teacher evaluation, as early as 2012–13 for some districts with all districts across the state implementing a new system by 2016–17. Though Illinois did not receive Race to the Top funds, the teacher evaluation legislation still stands.[8]

Evaluation Systems Across the Country Are Changing

Traditional Evaluation	Evidence-Based Evaluation
Single time point for classroom observation	Multiple time points for classroom observation
Use of "checklist" tools (strength/weakness, yes/no)	Use of rubrics that define instructional improvement on a continuum
Single observer	Multiple observers
High performance ratings given to almost all of the teachers	Variation in performance ratings among teachers
Does not include student outcomes	Links teacher effectiveness to student performance

The Chicago Context

Chicago's efforts to revamp teacher evaluation preceded the state and national push. A pilot evaluation system using a standards-based classroom observation rubric was implemented starting in 2008 under former CPS chief Arne Duncan, who is now U.S. Secretary of Education. That pilot system is the focus of this report.

Traditional Evaluation in Chicago

The traditional teacher evaluation system has been used by CPS for 30 years. Using an observation checklist, principals rate teacher performance in a number of areas as a strength, a weakness, or does not apply. The checklist does not include a definition of a strength or weakness. (The full checklist can be found in Appendix B.) At the end of each school year, principals provide teachers with a final performance evaluation rating—though there was no official guidance on how the observation checklist, or other evidence about teacher practice, related to that final rating.

These evaluation practices came under scrutiny when The New Teacher Project (TNTP) released a report on the district's teacher hiring, assignment, and transfer policies.[9] The report concluded that neither principals nor teachers perceived the checklist system to be meaningful or fair. Additionally, the checklist system did not lead to the identification or removal of low-performing teachers. In fact, teachers were only rarely identified as Unsatisfactory (0.3 percent) or even Satisfactory (7 percent), meaning 93 percent of the district's teachers were Excellent or Superior according to the checklist evaluation system.

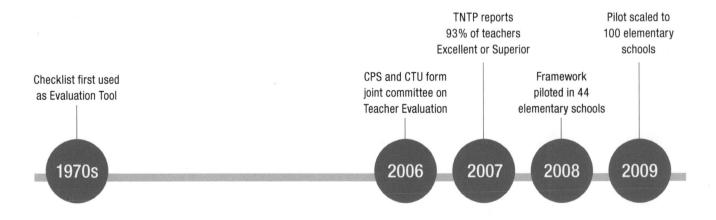

A New Approach to Evaluation—the Excellence in Teaching Pilot

In the summer of 2008, after collaborating with the Chicago Teachers Union for about two years, CPS launched the Excellence in Teaching Pilot, an initiative focused on instructional improvement through the use of an evaluation rubric that clearly defines the components of effective teaching. This rubric guided classroom observations and conferences between principals and teachers. The district set these pilot goals:

- Improve teaching and learning in the school district
- Develop a stronger professional learning climate among teachers and principals
- Foster a constructive—rather than punitive—climate around teacher evaluation

The first year of the pilot, 2008–09, included 44 elementary schools. Participation was scaled up to 101 elementary schools in 2009–10. The pilot consisted of training and support for principals, as well as training for teachers; principal observations of teaching practice formally conducted twice a year using the Danielson Framework; and conferences between the principal and teacher to discuss teaching practice. The conferences occurred before and after the formal classroom observation. In this report, we present findings on principal observation ratings and principal-teacher conferences.

Principals used the Charlotte Danielson Framework for Teaching to guide their note taking during classroom observations, as well as to focus their conferences with teachers. In Chicago, administrators conducted two formal observations during the school year using the Framework.

COMPONENTS OF CLASSROOM OBSERVATIONS FOR EXCELLENCE IN TEACHING PILOT

1. Pre-observation conference (15–25 minutes)
2. Classroom observation (a lesson, 30–60 minutes)
3. Administrators match their classroom observation notes to the Framework rubric in order to choose a level of performance for each of 10 components (45 minutes)
4. Post-observation conference (20–30 minutes)

Principals were expected to hold conferences with the teacher both before and after the observation. The pre-observation component was not required under the previous CPS evaluation system, though a few principals said they had always used pre-conferences. The district also provided forms for the teacher to fill out to guide the conferences.

Charlotte Danielson's Framework for Teaching

Originally developed in 1996, the Framework is used nationally to document and develop teaching practice. In Chicago, modified versions of the Danielson Framework have been used in a variety of initiatives, such as mentoring new teachers and evaluating teacher performance in a pay-for-performance pilot program.[10] Illinois has recently adopted a version of the Danielson Framework as the state's default observation rubric, although individual districts are able to choose a different tool. Other states (e.g., Idaho and Delaware) and districts (e.g., Cincinnati) also use versions of the Danielson Framework.

THE FRAMEWORK DIVIDES TEACHING INTO FOUR DOMAINS:

1. Planning and Preparation
2. Classroom Environment
3. Instruction
4. Professional Responsibilities

Domains 1 and 4 cover aspects of the teaching profession that occur outside the classroom, while Domains 2 and 3 address aspects that are directly observable in classroom teaching. Domains 2 and 3 are also the focus of the reliability and validity study because these domains were the emphasis of the pilot. (See Table 1 for a list of the components in Domains 2 and 3.)

The Framework is a rubric that delineates four levels of performance, or what we refer to as ratings, for each component. Each component has a detailed rubric that specifies rating criteria. A general description of the rating scale along with a rubric from a sample component, Using Questioning and Discussion Techniques, is shown in Table 2. (See Appendix A for the modified Danielson Framework rubric.)

TABLE 1

Components of Charlotte Danielson's Framework for Teaching

Domain 2: The Classroom Environment	Domain 3: Instruction
Creating an Environment of Respect and Rapport	Communicating With Students
Establishing a Culture for Learning	Using Questioning and Discussion Techniques
Managing Classroom Procedures	Engaging Students in Learning
Managing Student Behavior	Using Assessment in Instruction
Organizing Physical Space	Demonstrating Flexibility and Responsiveness

TABLE 2

Example of a rubric for one component: 3B. Using Questioning and Discussion Techniques

Level of Performance/Rating	General Description	Specific Rubric for 3B: Using Questioning and Discussion Techniques
Unsatisfactory	Teaching is below the standard of "do no harm" and requires immediate intervention.	Teacher's questions are low-level or inappropriate, eliciting limited student participation and recitation rather than discussion.
Basic	Teacher understands the components of teaching, but implementation is sporadic.	Some of the teacher's questions elicit a thoughtful response, but most are low-level, posed in rapid succession. Teacher attempts to engage all students in the discussion are only partially successful.
Proficient	Teacher has mastered the work of teaching.	Most of the teacher's questions elicit a thoughtful response, and the teacher allows sufficient time for students to answer. All students participate in the discussion, with the teacher stepping aside when appropriate.
Distinguished	Teacher has established a community of learners with students assuming responsibility for their own learning.	Questions reflect high expectations and are culturally and developmentally appropriate. Students formulate many of the high-level questions and ensure that all voices are heard.

Study Design and Data

CPS and the Consortium on Chicago School Research at the University of Chicago Urban Education Institute (CCSR) worked closely to design the rollout of the pilot. CPS selected four elementary school areas of the district to pilot the Danielson Framework. In those four areas, CCSR randomly selected half of the schools to participate in the pilot in 2008–09. The schools not selected began using the system one year later, in 2009–10. By randomly selecting schools, we ensured that findings regarding implementation would be generalizable to other elementary schools across the city. CCSR also randomly selected teachers within those schools for simultaneous classroom observation by the principal and an external observer. Random selection of teachers ensured that findings about teaching practice

and use of the Framework tool to measure teaching practice would be generalizable to elementary school teachers across the city.

To determine reliability, we utilized "matched" observations of teachers where two raters simultaneously observed teachers. One of the raters was usually the principal (but sometimes the assistant principal), and the other rater was one of three highly trained external observers.[11] The principal and the observer entered and left the classroom at the same time, and they assigned their ratings independently without discussing the lesson. We used the ratings from these classroom observations to determine if an individual principal applied the Framework ratings consistently.

To determine validity, we used principal observation of teachers who had math and/or reading value-added

Research Questions

1. **What are the characteristics of principal ratings of teaching practice?**

   a. Do evaluators rate the same lesson in the same way? Do principals rate teaching practice consistently across schools?

   b. Are the classroom observation ratings valid measures of teaching practice? Is there a relationship between ratings and student learning outcomes?

2. **What are principal and teacher perceptions of the evaluation tool and conferences?**

   a. Do participants find the system to be useful? To be fair?

   b. What is the perceived impact on teacher practice?

3. **What factors facilitated or impeded implementation of the teacher evaluation system?**

Quantitative Research

Data Source	Sample Size
Reliability observations—principal and external observer ratings of the same lesson	499 observations 257 teachers
Validity observations—principal ratings	955 observations 501 teachers
Teacher-level value-added measures	417 reading teachers 340 math teachers
CCSR principal survey (spring 2009)	37 pilot principals 37 control principals

Note: See Chapters 2, 3, and 5, as well as Appendix D, for details on data, methodology, and findings regarding validity and reliability of the classroom observation rubric.

Qualitative Research

	Data Source	Sample Size
Data Collected Across All Pilot Schools	Principal Interviews (Cohort 1)	39
	Teacher Interviews (Cohort 1)	26
	Principal Focus Groups (Cohorts 1 and 2)	23
Data Collected From Eight Case Study Schools	Principal Interviews	8 Principals x 3 Time Points
	Assistant Principal Interviews	8
	Teacher Focus Groups	14
	Observation Series: Pre-Conference, Classroom Observation, Post-Conference, and Teacher Debrief	21

Note: More detailed methodology and findings about implementation at the school level, including principal engagement and coaching conversations, are discussed in Chapters 4 and 5 and in Appendix E.

measures from CPS. We compared teachers' observation ratings and value-added measures to establish the relationship between the two for each component of the Framework for reading and math.

Qualitative data collection and analysis provided answers to the second and third research questions. In 2008–09, we asked the first cohort of principals about the Danielson Framework, training and support, conferences with teachers, and logistics regarding school-level implementation. Analysis of the interviews resulted in the principal engagement findings. In 2009–10, we conducted case studies in eight of the pilot elementary schools—the case study schools were selected based on the principal's level of engagement, so we studied schools that ranged from low buy-in to high engagement around the pilot work. The case study analysis led to the findings regarding principal coaching during conferences, as well as the school vignettes of implementation.

Chapter 2

Validity of Observation Ratings

This chapter provides detailed information about the relationship between classroom observation ratings and student learning. Specifically, the chapter explores whether teachers who receive higher ratings also tend to have students who achieve greater test score growth. We refer to the relationship between observation ratings and student learning as validity because a "valid" evaluation system should rate teachers based on the factors that improve learning. A valid system, for example, might rate teachers based on how well they explain course material, while an invalid system might rate teachers on more arbitrary factors (e.g., appearance). And while we would not expect to see any relationship between test score gains and appearance, we might expect to see a positive relationship between test scores gains and asking challenging questions. This chapter considers whether principals rated teaching practice validly in the Chicago pilot, and, more specifically, whether the Danielson Framework, the observation tool utilized in the Excellence in Teaching Pilot, is a valid measure of teaching practice.

KEY FINDINGS ON VALIDITY

- There is a strong relationship between classroom observation ratings and value-added measures, and the relationship holds for math and reading test scores.

- In the classrooms of highly rated teachers, students showed the most growth; in the classrooms of teachers with low observation ratings, students showed the least growth.

Validity: The Relationship Between Classroom Observation Ratings and Student Achievement

There is a national push to evaluate teachers based on the growth their students make on standardized tests, resulting in the increasing popularity of value-added models. There are many approaches to value-added modeling, which range in complexity, but the goal is simply to identify the effect of an individual teacher, or an individual school, on student learning.

One limitation of the value-added approach is that most teachers do not teach a subject or grade level that is currently tested. Another limitation is that some of the standardized assessments currently given to students were not designed to measure student growth. Given these and other limitations, establishing that a classroom observation rubric is a valid way to measure teaching practice becomes crucial. If there is an established relationship between classroom observation ratings and student learning, then classroom observation ratings can provide a good indicator of teacher quality for teachers in untested grades.

In this study, we empirically tested the relationship between teaching practice (as measured by the Danielson Framework ratings) and student learning (see the sidebar What to Know About CPS Value-Added Measures and Validity). If the Framework and the value-added indicators are valid, we expect, for example, that the teachers with the highest classroom observation ratings are the same teachers with the highest value-added indicators.

To test validity, we ran a statistical model comparing the Framework ratings to the value-added measures. We did this for each component of the Framework for reading and math. These models resulted in 1) the average value-added measure for teachers at each of the four levels of the rating scale, and 2) the significance of the relationship between ratings and value-added measures. (See Appendix D for more technical information on the validity testing.)

There is a strong relationship between classroom observation ratings and test score growth. Across almost all of the Framework components, teachers with the lowest observation ratings also have the lowest value-added measures—and the value-added measures increase

What to Know About CPS Value-Added Measures and Validity

- Developed by the Value Added Research Center (VARC) at the University of Wisconsin[12]

- Measures only available for grades 4–8 reading and math teachers

- A value-added measure:
  - Of zero indicates that the teacher's students grew an average amount over the school year
  - Below zero indicates that the teacher's students had below average growth
  - Above zero indicates that the teacher's students had above average growth

- Models take into account student demographics, daily attendance, and mobility

In Chicago, all teachers in grades 4–8 English language arts and/or mathematics have value-added indicators. To be included in our analysis, an individual teacher needed to have both 1) classroom observation ratings from the principal, and 2) a value-added indicator. This leaves us with a sample of 955 principal observations of 501 teachers. The teachers in our sample have slightly higher value-added measures than the whole population of teachers in CPS, more so in reading than in math, though the average value-added measure for these teachers is still close to zero. The most common Danielson Framework rating for teachers in the sample is Proficient.

as the teacher's rating increases.[13] In other words, on average, a teacher with an Unsatisfactory rating has a lower value-added indicator than a teacher with a Basic rating, a teacher with a Basic rating has a lower value-added measure than a teacher with a Proficient rating, and a teacher with a Proficient rating has a lower value-added measure than a teacher with a Distinguished rating. This pattern generally holds across the components, suggesting that the Framework is measuring teaching practice in a valid way. This relationship between Framework ratings and value-added measures is statistically significant for all of the components. Other researchers looking at the relationship between Framework ratings and value-added measures in Cincinnati have produced similar results.[14]

The results for math are comparable to reading. For almost all of the components, on average, teachers who receive lower classroom observation ratings also have lower value-added measures. One difference between reading and math is that teachers who received a Basic rating generally have a below average value-added measure, whereas teachers with Proficient ratings have students with close to average gains in test scores.

In other words, a math teacher and a reading teacher may have the same classroom observation ratings, but the math teacher will generally have a lower value-added measure than the reading teacher unless he/she is Proficient. Despite this difference between reading and math, there is still a significant difference in the math value-added measures of teachers with lower ratings of classroom practice than with higher ratings of classroom practice. This difference holds across all 10 components. Again, this finding suggests that the Framework ratings are a valid measure of classroom practice. (See Appendix D for average value-added measures for all components of the Danielson Framework, including results from significance testing.)

A Note on Data Limitations

Due to data limitations, we may be underestimating the relationship between ratings and value-added indicators. While researchers and practitioners have highlighted issues with using value-added measures for evaluation purposes, we want to mention some problems that relate specifically to limitations in data

FIGURE 1

Teachers with higher Framework ratings had higher value-added measures

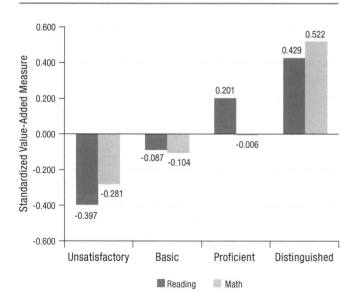

HOW TO READ FIGURE 1

Figure 1 provides an example for one of the Framework components: Demonstrating Flexibility and Responsiveness (3E). Reading value-added measures are in purple, and math value-added measures are in gray. The number indicates the average value-added measure for teachers who received a particular Framework rating. For example, teachers who received an Unsatisfactory rating in Demonstrating Flexibility and Responsiveness had an average reading value-added measure of -0.397 and an average math value-added measure of -0.281 (about one-third of a standard deviation below normal).

In reading, the average value-added measure for teachers with an Unsatisfactory rating is well below zero, whereas the value-added measure for teachers with a Basic hovers close to zero. This means that, on average, teachers who received an Unsatisfactory rating of their classroom practice had below average student growth compared to other similar students. In general, teachers rated Basic had average or just below average student growth, and teachers rated Proficient or Distinguished had above average student growth.

systems and in identifying which students are actually taught by which teachers.[15] Evaluating teachers based on the achievement of their students, as measured by standardized tests, means that districts must be able to identify which teachers teach which students. Elementary schools are relying more and more heavily on team teaching and arrangements that allow for more differentiation of instruction for students. These flexible arrangements make it difficult to pinpoint—at least with the current data systems—which teacher is teaching each individual student and how to attribute student growth accordingly. While we do not know the rate at which elementary schools are using these strategies, we do know that they are common. And the problem of matching students to teachers is a bigger one in schools that use flexible teaching arrangements to a greater extent.

The classroom observation ratings also have limitations. (See Chapter 3 for details on reliability.) In the validity analysis, we use the raw ratings that principals assigned, rather than a statistically adjusted rating, because that is how this teacher evaluation rating system (or any other) would be implemented. If the value-added indicators measured student growth perfectly and if the classroom observation measures were completely devoid of any individual rater bias, we suspect the relationship between the two measures would be even stronger.

Chapter 3

Reliability of Observation Ratings

In addition to validity, another important consideration when designing an evaluation system is whether teachers will be rated consistently. That is, will teachers demonstrating the same levels of proficiency receive the same ratings? We refer to this relationship as "reliability." To measure reliability, we compared principal and observer ratings of the same lesson.

In our reliability analyses, we are not assuming that the principal is right or wrong in assigning ratings—nor are we assuming the observer is always right. We are simply comparing principal and observer ratings. To measure reliability, we made a direct comparison of principal and observer ratings of the same lesson. Our analysis allows us to say if principals and observers agree on teacher ratings across all components of the Framework and at all levels of the rating scale. It is possible that problems with inter-rater reliability can be somewhat alleviated through training and support. If principals consistently rate a component lower or higher than the observers, the district can provide more support to principals in how to rate teaching practice in that area.

KEY FINDINGS ON RELIABILITY

- Principals rated teaching practice reliably at the low end and the middle of the scale.

- However, they were more likely to rate practice as Distinguished when observers rated practice as Proficient.

- Most principals agreed with external observers when it came to rating teaching practice, though 11 percent of principals consistently gave lower ratings than the observers and 17 percent consistently gave higher ratings than the observers.

An Overview of the Ratings Data

Table 3 and Figure 2 show how principals and observers rated teaching practice. Table 3 shows the overall distribution of ratings awarded to teachers in the sample across all components of the Framework, and Figure 2 breaks the information down component by component. While principals and observers gave similar proportions of Unsatisfactory and Basic ratings, there is a noticeable difference between the proportion of Distinguished ratings given by principals and those given by observers. These ratings form the backbone of the reliability and validity analyses.

TABLE 3

Distribution of ratings for principals and observers

Rating	Principal (N=4,747 ratings)	Observer (N=4,852 ratings)
Distinguished	803 (17%)	157 (3%)
Proficient	2,530 (53%)	3,259 (67%)
Basic	1,291 (27%)	1,343 (28%)
Unsatisfactory	123 (3%)	93 (2%)

FIGURE 2

Principals and observers gave similar proportions of Unsatisfactory and Basic ratings in most of the components, though principals were more likely to call practice Distinguished

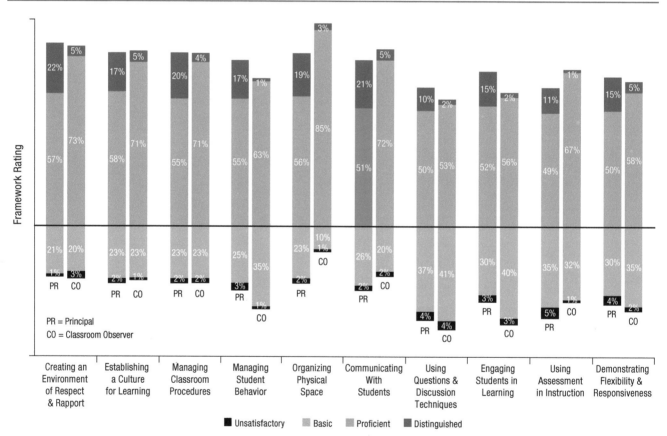

HOW TO READ FIGURE 2

Figure 2 shows the distribution of ratings—by principals and observers—for each of the 10 components across teachers in the pilot schools. Below the line in black and gray and purple are the Unsatisfactory and Basic ratings, and above the line in light purple and dark purple are Proficient and Distinguished. Principal and observer bars in which the colors generally line up, beginning and ending at the same level, indicate that principals and observers gave similar proportions of Framework ratings for that component (see Managing Classroom Procedures, for example). Bars in which the colors do not coincide indicate that principals and observers gave different proportions of ratings. For example, with Organizing Physical Space, principals gave more Basic ratings while observers gave more Proficient ratings.

Figure 2 shows the ratings that principals and observers assigned to the teachers in the sample. In three of the components, you can see relatively large differences between Basic and Proficient ratings—Managing Student Behavior (2D), Organizing Physical Space (2E), and Engaging Students in Learning (3C). With Managing Student Behavior and Engaging Students in Learning, the principals tended to assign higher ratings than the observers, whereas with Organizing Physical Space the principals often rated lower than the observers. Across all of the components, principals were more likely to call practice Distinguished that observers rated as Proficient.

Figure 2 also provides more general information about teaching practice according to both principals and observers. Teachers received lower ratings in the Instruction components (the five sets of bars on the right) than in the Classroom Environment domain (the five sets of bars on the left). You can see this in the figure because the bars for the Instruction components hang farther below the line that separates Basic from Proficient ratings.

Inter-Rater Reliability—Agreement in Ratings Between Principals and Observers

The ratings in Figure 2 provide a sense of the differences and similarities of principal and observer ratings. These ratings are the descriptive data that serve as the basis for our statistical modeling. The statistical models allow for direct comparisons of principal and observer ratings of the same lesson for 501 observations of 257 teachers, and the results indicate where principal-observer differences are significant and where they generally agree with each other. (See Appendix D for details on the statistical models.)

We isolated each part of the rating scale to determine if principals and observers rated consistently across the four categories of performance in the Framework, or if there were differences in reliability at each level of the scale. (The low end is Unsatisfactory and Basic, the middle is Basic and Proficient, and the high end is Proficient and Distinguished.) The statistical models are structured to make direct comparisons of a principal's ratings and an observer's ratings of the same lesson.

Overall, principals rated Unsatisfactory teaching practices reliably. Principals and observers generally agreed when practice was Unsatisfactory. The same is true for the middle of the scale. That means, in general, principals and observers were able to agree upon Unsatisfactory versus Basic practice (as shown by the Low End Scale bar, which is not significantly different from an odds ratio of 1.00, in Figure 3) and Basic versus Proficient practice (as shown by the Middle Scale bar in Figure 3).

Given this finding, the Framework appears to be a reliable tool at the low end of the rating scale. Reliability at the low end of the scale is critical if district leadership intends to use the Framework ratings to identify low-quality instruction, remove ineffective teachers, or assign low-performing teachers to professional development. During a formal observation using the Framework, principals assigned at least one Unsatisfactory rating to 8 percent of teachers in the sample. The definition of Unsatisfactory practice, according to the Framework, is doing academic harm to students and requires immediate intervention.

Across all components and observations, principals were more likely than observers to rate teaching practice Distinguished. While reliability is high at the low end of the rating scale, principals assigned the Distinguished rating more often than the observers did across all 10 components of teaching. Of the 257 teachers observed simultaneously by the principal and observer, 52 percent received at least one Distinguished rating from principals, but only 24 percent received a Distinguished rating from observers. Across all components, principals were also significantly more likely to call practice Distinguished when observers rated the same instruction as Proficient (as shown by the top High End Scale bar in Figure 3).

In interviews, principals provided a rationale for this finding. They acknowledged that for some teachers they intentionally rated practice that should have been Proficient as Distinguished because of the need to preserve relationships with teachers who had previously received the high evaluation ratings. One principal said, "I am not going to get in a big fight between these two things (Proficient versus Distinguished) because what good does it do? You just ruin your relationship with the teacher. It is much better to coach them than [explain] what the differences are between Proficient and Distinguished."

It is important to note that when comparing principal and observer ratings, we are not implying that the principal or the observer is "right." While the principals used the Distinguished rating more often, these teachers did have higher value-added measures than the teachers the principals rated as Proficient. This suggests either that principals are correctly identifying Distinguished practice or that they used historical knowledge of the teacher (unknown to the observer and outside of the evidence of the classroom observation) to form a better picture of teacher effectiveness. (See Chapter 2 for details.)

Some differences in principal and observer ratings are explained by a teacher's previous evaluation rating. When principals entered classrooms to conduct observations for formal evaluation, they were expected to set aside preconceived notions about teachers, to collect evidence in a systematic way, and to use that evidence to determine a teacher's evaluation rating. This was a much more complex task than what principals had been asked to do in the past. The quantitative analysis revealed that the ratings principals assigned to teachers on previous evaluations mattered, especially if that teacher had received high evaluation ratings in the past. For example, if a teacher had previously received the highest rating on the checklist, the principal using the Framework sometimes rated that teacher's practice higher than the observer.

When we took into account teachers' previous evaluation ratings in the statistical models, much of the variation between principal and observer ratings disappeared. This suggests that principals may have taken previous evaluation ratings into account when assigning new ratings. One example of this is evident in Figure 3. When we compare the purple bars, we see that the difference in principal and observer ratings at the high end of the scale is quite large. However, after controlling for a teacher's prior evaluation rating, the

FIGURE 3

Principals were far more likely than external observers to give teachers the highest rating

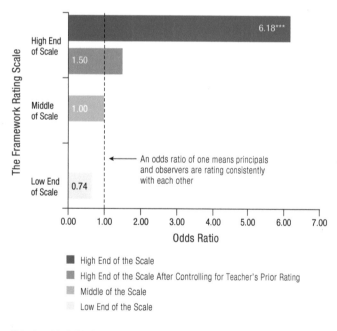

- High End of the Scale
- High End of the Scale After Controlling for Teacher's Prior Rating
- Middle of the Scale
- Low End of the Scale

Note: Asterisks (***) indicate a significant difference between principal and observer ratings with principals more likely to assign a higher rating at the .01 level. No asterisks means that the relationship was not significant. In other words, principals and observers rated lessons similarly. We controlled for the subject area of the lesson, grade level of the lesson, tenure status, and *prior evaluation rating* on the CPS checklist, as well as the year of the observation and the year that the principal began using the Framework to assign ratings.

TABLE 4

How to interpret odds ratios

The Odds Ratio	What It Means	Example From Figure 3
Equals One	The principal and the observer give the same rating	Middle of the scale—the odds of a principal giving a Proficient rating rather than a Basic rating, compared to the observer, are 1 to 1
Is Greater Than One	The principal gives a higher rating than the observer	High end of the scale (highly significant)—the odds of a principal giving a Distinguished rating rather than a Proficient rating, compared to the observer, are 6 to 1
Is Less Than One	The principal gives a lower rating than the observer	Low end of the scale (not significantly different from one)—the odds of a principal giving a Basic rating rather than an Unsatisfactory rating, compared to the observer, are 3 to 4

difference diminishes and is no longer statistically significant. Another interpretation is that principals' prior knowledge of teachers enables them to rate teaching practice more accurately than the observers. Because we saw a strong relationship between principal ratings of teachers and value-added measures, there is evidence that principals are accurately assessing teaching practice, even at the high end of the scale.

Figure 3 shows the variation between principal and observer ratings of the same lesson. The figure displays the odds that a principal gives a certain rating compared to the odds that an observer gives that same rating (i.e., the odds ratio—see Table 4 for more information on how to interpret odds ratios). **If principals and observers are assigning the same ratings, we expect the odds ratio to equal 1.**

Limited Principal Understanding of How to Rate Practice: Walton Elementary School

The example of Walton School makes the case for the importance of reliably rating teaching practice. If teachers do not believe that their principal is rating accurately, the potential of the evaluation system is stifled.

The principal resisted the pilot evaluation system. In the first year of the pilot, Ms. Cooper, the principal, expressed negative sentiments about the Framework and the new teacher evaluation system, stating that rating teaching practice using the Framework was "a lot more work." She struggled with choosing a rating and was often torn between Basic and Proficient. She also perceived that teachers put on a performance when she came to visit, and that the Framework did not reveal their "real teaching." Ms. Cooper said that the new evaluation process overwhelmed her. The print on the Framework summary pages was too small to read, there were too many components of teaching practice to rate, and the technology principals used to enter ratings was difficult. By the end of the second year, she said, "It still just confused me."

The teachers had high hopes for the pilot, but they recognized the principal's limitations in using the Framework. Teachers at Walton were generally positive about the Charlotte Danielson Framework, but they were negative about the way it was being used in their school. One teacher described the tool as "having powerful potential," but thought the principal's limited use "made it just as subjective as the old tool." One teacher said she had "corrected the principal several times in her misinterpretations of the Framework." This teacher explained that, while she was not an expert in the Framework, she believed she "knew more than the principal just by reading it through."

There was a sense among interviewed teachers that the Framework had caused problems in the school because the principal was simply not using it fairly. Teachers thought the principal had good intentions, but she "just didn't have the instructional knowledge to use the Framework well." Teachers expressed that the implementation of the teacher evaluation pilot at the school was "weak at best." They felt initially hopeful when the pilot was introduced into the school and were excited about the training. "I hoped for the best, but it just didn't go that deep," one teacher stated. The teachers came in with high expectations of what the tool would accomplish and, thus, were "tremendously disappointed when the Framework was used poorly."

The principal's lack of knowledge of the Framework and inability to rate teaching practice led teachers to believe the pilot evaluation was subjective. Teachers perceived that the principal's leadership capacity and knowledge of instructional practice was limited. The principal herself admitted that this kept her from being able to deeply understand and use the Danielson Framework. Teachers became disenchanted and frustrated as they realized the Framework would not be used in a deep way. Many disengaged from the process as a result. As the second year of the pilot closed, both Ms. Cooper and the teachers expressed deep concerns about the ability of the teacher evaluation pilot to promote instructional and school improvement.

Rater Severity

Another set of analyses focused on how individual principals rated in comparison to the observers across multiple observations of teachers within their school, allowing us to identify individual principals who regularly rated teaching practice differently than the observers. Lenient principals consistently rated teaching practice higher than the observers did, while severe principals rated teaching practice lower than the observers. The following findings provide information on rater severity.

Most principals were on par with the observers. Comparing principal and observer ratings using a measurement model, we determined which principals regularly rated lower than the observers (11 percent of principals), which principals were generally in line with the observers (72 percent of principals), and which principals regularly rated higher than the observers (17 percent of principals). Figure 4 shows the distribution of principal severity across the two years.

Figures 5 and 6 are examples of classroom observation ratings from a more severe and a more lenient

FIGURE 4

When rating teaching practice, most principals generally agreed with the observers

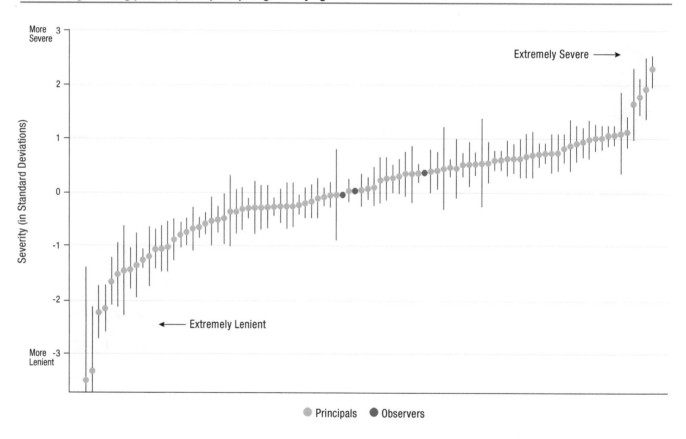

Principals ● Observers

HOW TO READ FIGURE 4

Each dot on the figure represents a rater: purple dots are observers, and gray dots are principals. Data used to construct this figure consist of 166 observations from each of the three observers and, on average, six observations from each of the 84 principals (some principals did not enter observation data). The lines above and below the dot are error bars. Longer bars mean we are less confident about that principal's severity; the true severity measure could fall anywhere within that bar. Error could come from two sources:

1) we have little classroom observation data from the rater, and/or 2) the principal was inconsistent in how he/she assigned Framework ratings compared to the observers. Most of the principals are close to the observers in terms of severity (within one standard deviation of the observers). There were more extremely lenient principals (shown on the far left) in the sample than extremely severe principals (shown on the far right).

principal. The ratings are coded from Unsatisfactory to Distinguished. These figures provide an example of what severity and leniency mean for an individual teacher.

The teacher in Figure 5 a consistently received Basic ratings from his/her principal and Proficient ratings from the external observer—except in Demonstrating Flexibility and Responsiveness (3E), where the principal and observer rated this component as Basic.

Figure 6 shows the classroom observation ratings for a teacher from a principal who was identified as a lenient rater in our analysis and the external observer. Sometimes the principal and observer agreed on ratings of teacher practice—where the lines overlap and the dots are on top of each other. However, with half of the components, the principal gave higher ratings than the observer.

FIGURE 5

This is an example of a severe principal who generally gave lower ratings than the observer

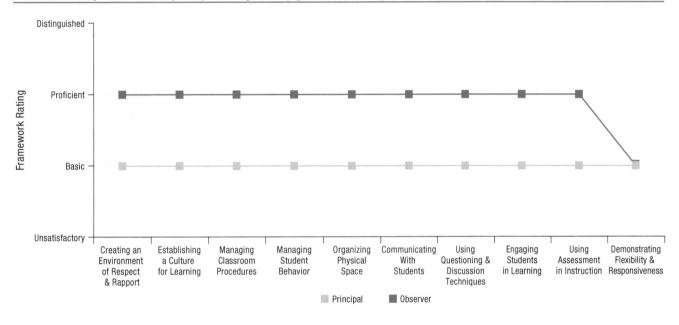

FIGURE 6

This is an example of a lenient principal who generally gave higher ratings than the observer

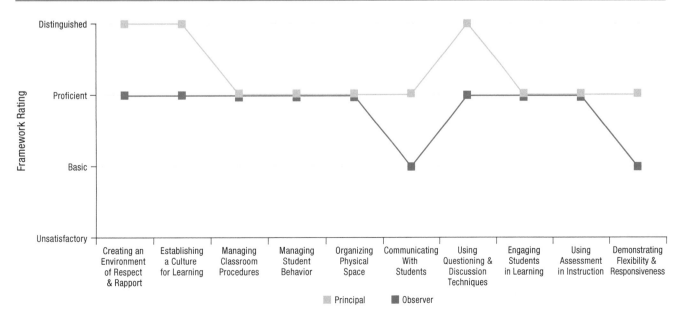

Chapter 4

Principals and Teachers
Talk About Instruction

One goal for adopting the Danielson Framework was to establish a shared language around instructional improvement. While the rubric provides a tool for rating teaching, the conferences were intended to be the lever for translating the ratings into changes in instructional practice. Based on the rating and evidence generated during the observation, a principal and a teacher could use the conference to discuss specific ways, for example, to improve student engagement or to develop strategies for managing student behavior. As such, the pre- and post-observation conferences were a central component of the pilot evaluation system in Chicago. In this chapter, we explore the conversations principals and teachers had about instruction.

KEY FINDINGS ON CONVERSATIONS ABOUT INSTRUCTION

- Principals and teachers thought the conferences they had about instruction using Charlotte Danielson's Framework for Teaching were:
    - More reflective than those they had using the CPS checklist
    - Based on a shared language about instructional practice and improvement
    - Evidence-based, which reduced subjectivity
- Positive attitudes about conferences were dependent on principals' skills and buy-in.
- Our observations of the conferences revealed that the quality of the conversations could be improved and that principals need more support in engaging in deep coaching conversations. Conversations were:
    - Dominated by principal talk
    - Driven by low-level questions, although this varied across principals and teachers

District Expectations for Conferences

Principals were expected to hold conferences with the teacher both before and after the observation. The pre-observation component was not required under the traditional district evaluation system, though a few principals said they had always used pre-conferences. District staff also provided forms for the teacher to fill out to guide the conferences.

The district's theory was that when conferences were supported by the use of a rigorous evaluation rubric, the conversation would be more intentionally focused on instruction, elevate the professional dialogue in schools, and allow teachers and principals to be honest and reflective. At a training session, Charlotte Danielson told CPS principals that what matters most in the evaluation process is that principals and teachers are talking to each other about instruction. One principal said the tenor of the conferences should move from "how did I do?" to "how do I get better?" In the end, these conversations were intended to promote meaningful improvements in teaching practice.

The District Wanted Teachers and Principals to Talk About...

- How the lesson relates to the curriculum and the sequence of learning for the class

- Characteristics of students in the class and how their individual needs varied

- The goals for student learning

- How the teacher will engage students

- How the teacher will differentiate instruction

- How the teacher will assess learning

- If and how the teacher departed from the lesson plan

- What changes the teacher would make if he/she could re-teach the lesson

Principal and Teacher Perceptions: Using Evaluation to Focus on Instruction

Principals and teachers were generally positive about the conversations they had about instruction using Charlotte Danielson's Framework for Teaching.

Principals and teachers reported that conferences were more structured and focused on instruction than in past evaluations and that the Framework provided a common language to talk about instruction. Principals and teachers moved from using an observation checklist to one that defined instructional practice developmentally based on what principals observed in the classroom. The Danielson observation tool required principals to document what they saw in the classroom as the basis for their ratings and for their conferences. It makes sense, then, that teachers and principals reported that conferences were more structured and focused on instruction when using this evidence-based tool.

Principals reflected on conferences they had conducted in the past and suggested that using Charlotte Danielson's Framework for Teaching changed the "content and tone" of the discussion. "The conversation is entirely different. My conversation before was 'you were tardy,' 'you didn't turn in your lesson plans,' all those kinds of things. Now I think this conversation is about good instruction," one principal explained. Many teachers said the Framework gave their conversations focus and direction. The ratings rubric helped them be "on the same page" as their principals regarding the definitions of the ratings and components. One teacher said, "The domains [of the Framework] give you something to reflect on and talk about with the principal, and...we have something concrete that you value."

Both principals and teachers noted increased reflection on instructional practice. One goal of instructional coaching is that teachers will become more reflective practitioners.[16] Most principals stated that the pre- and post-conferences using Charlotte Danielson's Framework for Teaching led to more reflective discussion. "Conversations were deepened because the Framework has explicit goals for improving instruction," one principal stated. Teachers also felt like the conferencing process made them more reflective on their own teaching practice. One teacher said, "I enjoyed the

Principals Liked the Conferences

- 89% agreed: the quality of conversations with teachers has improved

- 86% agreed: the Framework provides a common definition of high-quality teaching in their school

feedback from the principal, and I definitely got some ideas about some things that I was lacking.…It gets me thinking about how I'm approaching the class, and how my lesson fits into the structure of the entire year, and the purpose of it."

Many of the principals specifically mentioned that the new system facilitated reflective discussions in a way that conferences using the old checklist system had not. For example, one principal said about one of his teachers, "She didn't see the value of it last year, but this year…I don't know if we ever would have had that conversation before."

One specific benefit of pre-conferences is the additional reflection and time allocated to planning a lesson. Roughly half of the principals suggested that the use of the pre-conference led to better preparation on the part of the teachers. "It made them plan. It made them think," one principal stated. "We talked together about the lesson and she revised it on the spot, making the planning process deeper and more reflective," another principal stated.

Evidence played a significant role in the conferences and decreased subjectivity during conversations about teaching practice, according to principals and teachers. A major emphasis in the implementation of the evaluation system and in principal training was to collect evidence and then to place teachers on the rubric using that evidence. The goal was to promote fairness and remove subjectivity from the rating process. Evidence might consist of statements such as: "Ms. Smith told Adam to be quiet five times." To compare, a more subjective version of that statement might read: "Ms. Smith wasn't able to keep Adam on task."

In general, administrators felt that using the Framework to evaluate teacher practice structured their conversations with teachers, allowing them to identify specific areas for instructional improvement. One administrator explained that having evidence made "it easier to talk about the good and the bad." Evidence-based observations also helped to remove some of the emotion from the evaluation process. When talking to teachers who were unhappy with their ratings, or who had received Unsatisfactory ratings, one administrator said, "You will have enough evidence to support what you're saying." Evidence-based feedback during post-conferences gave teachers "the opportunity to look at themselves and what their performance truly looked like."

Positive attitudes about conferences were dependent on principal skills and buy-in. While most principals and teachers were positive about conferences, a small proportion of those we interviewed had mixed or negative perceptions. In particular, some principals thought that using the Framework resulted in conferences that took too much time. "I have to talk through all these components. Does the district think I have nothing else to do but observe and talk to teachers?" one principal asked. Teachers who were mixed or negative in their assessment of conferences were also often skeptical of their principal's ability to use the tool accurately or fairly. "The conference has potential. But my principal just read me the form while I sat there, and that was the end of it." This is described in more detail in the case study about Walton School in the previous chapter. Similarly, a small portion of teachers reported that the new tool and conversations using it didn't reduce subjectivity. This was described as a difficulty that was not inherent in the Framework for Teaching but was in the way it was used by principals in the conferences. "There were ratings that he [the principal] didn't even have evidence for…or it was evidence from another teacher's classroom that he must have cut and pasted in the wrong place."

Assessing the Quality of Conversations Between Principals and Teachers

In this chapter, we explore the findings of our analysis of the observations of conversations about instruction between principals and teachers. We considered these data in two ways. First, we analyzed the types of questions principals asked teachers during conferences.

We use this to gauge the depth of the conversations. Second, we analyzed the proportion of time that principals talk versus the proportion of time teachers talk to gain an understanding of the give-and-take between principal and teacher, which we use as another measure of the quality of conversations.

We do not know the exact proportion of questions that should be high, medium, or low level in order to say that a principal was successfully engaging teachers in meaningful conversations about instruction. It is reasonable to expect that some low-level questions are appropriate, especially when framing or initiating a discussion. However, asking good questions is vital for fostering reflection and learning—this is true of both student and adult learners. While questioning is an important instructional strategy for teachers, it is also an important skill for principals who are trying to engage teachers in coaching conversations.

Very few (10 percent) of the questions principals asked teachers were at a high level. We categorized 300 principal questions from pre- and post-observation conferences with 21 teachers. We sorted principal questions into three categories: high-level, medium-level, and low-level. The criteria for these categories were based on the Danielson Framework's definition for teachers of what constitutes high-level and low-level questions.

The vast majority of principals' questions were of low or medium depth and failed to promote discussions about instruction as shown in Table 5.

The quality of questions depended on the principal, but also on the teacher. The level of questioning varied in two ways across the principals. First, there was variation in principal capacity to ask deep questions about instruction. Roughly half of the principals asked primarily low- and mid-level questions, while roughly the other half of the principals asked mostly mid- and high-level questions. Second, some principals changed the way they conducted conferences based on the teacher. Some principals noted that their teachers had varying abilities to engage in reflective conversation, so they adjusted the depth of their critique and questioning intentionally. For instance, one principal stated, "I only give each teacher what she can handle. With Ms. Sampson, I can just be honest. 'That was terrible. You need to differentiate.' With Ms. Ember, I have to stick to the basics: 'Did you cover the lesson you said you would cover?' Check."

Training for the new system was primarily focused on how to use the Framework and on how to give teachers fair ratings. While the coaching conversation with teachers around the observation was a topic in the training, many principals believed it was covered

TABLE 5

Principals generally asked questions that did not promote discussion about instruction

Level of Questioning	Rubric	Example From a Conference	Percent of Questions (N=300)
Low	Principal's question requires limited teacher response rather than discussion. The questions are generally focused on simple affirmation of principal perception, such as agreement with principal rating. The teacher response is often a single word and doesn't push principal interpretations.	I think this was a Basic because of the evidence I collected. Do you agree? Did you finish the lesson?	65%
Medium	Principal's question requires short teacher response. The questions are generally focused on completion of tasks and requirements. The teacher provides a brief response in explanation.	How did you fulfill the goals you set for this lesson? Which goals did you not meet?	25%
High	Principal's question requires extensive teacher response. The question and response reflect high expectations and require deep reflection about instructional practice. The principal and teacher push one another's interpretations.	What is the relationship between student engagement and classroom management in your teaching? What are some concrete steps you can take to improve each?	10%

inadequately. Some principals were uncertain about their role in the coaching process, struggling with how to frame and lead the conversations with teachers. Other principals found it challenging to engage in constructive conversations with teachers who had rarely reflected on their teaching. One principal described her uncertainty: "I'm not sure if I'm asking the right questions to bring teachers to that reflective state that we want them to be in." Another principal suggested that teachers did not necessarily know how to have the reflective conversation. He said, "Since I have a lot of new teachers, they're not sure how to do it. I'm not having that reflective conversation—I'm more leading, teaching, and directing." About half of the principals explicitly discussed their desire for training in this area.

Principals tended to dominate the conversations. One goal of coaching conversations is to have the teacher participate actively in the conversation. To assess whether teachers took an active role in these evaluation conferences, we analyzed who was doing the talking and who was doing the questioning—the principal, the teacher, or both. We found that principals drove the discussion the majority of the time: Their questions and comments took up roughly 75 percent of the conference, while teacher input accounted for just 25 percent.

Some conversations between principals and teachers were much more proportionate. These conversations were more dynamic, allowing the teacher to explain her/his viewpoint, discuss improvement strategies, and, in some cases, to challenge the principal's interpretation of the instructional practice. Conversations that were dominated by the principal tended to leave less room for the teacher to engage. Table 6 shows an example of a principal-dominated conversation, as well as one with more balanced/teacher-driven exchanges.

TABLE 6

Examples of principal-dominated and teacher-driven conversations

Conversation Snapshot: Principal Dominated	Conversation Snapshot: Balanced/Teacher Driven
Principal: So did you finish the lesson? Teacher: Yes. Principal: And tomorrow...onto the next one? Teacher: Right. Principal: Let me tell you my perceptions on this unit. The strengths were, many of the students were on task and focused. You followed your plan. You moved from one thing, one activity, to the next. The weakness seemed to be the students didn't know the purpose, the goal or reason, for what they were doing. Next time I will come in and look just at that...ask students what they are doing and why. Teacher: Okay. Principal: Because you see that part is important. Teachers think it is a small thing, but it isn't. It is critical. You can have all the best stuff in the world you are teaching, but students who don't know why won't get it. So would you agree, that is a Basic? Teacher: Yes, I will work on it. Principal: Great, because you are starting to get there. We have to keep moving forward and striving to improve. Teacher: Okay.	Principal: To begin with, can you tell me, in your own words, what was the goal of this lesson? What did you hope the students would get out of this? Teacher: I guess I hoped they would leave with a better understanding of inference. What is it, how can you recognize it in the text, what role does it play in storytelling? And I wanted them to be able to identify clues from the text to explain it to their partners. The piece you saw was just one aspect of a whole cluster of lessons focused on understanding text and textual analysis. I had a secondary goal of working on my pacing, both across the set of lessons and in a single class period. Principal: And in your opinion, how did it go? What did they get or not get? Strengths and weaknesses of this lesson? Why don't you start with the pacing goal and then talk about the inference goal? Teacher: I think my pacing was good on the set of lessons around these concepts. We moved through the pieces of information and the pace of the class period as well. Students were engaged. On the goal of learning inference as a part of this larger textual analysis lesson, I felt my effectiveness was mixed. I felt like maybe two-thirds of the students understood it. But one-third were lost. What did you think? Principal: I agree both with your assessment of the management piece and with your assessment of the inference part. That is why I gave you a Basic here and a Proficient here. Let's talk through each one separately, and I can show you the part of the observation where I found support for those ratings.

Contrasts in Instructional Coaching: The Cases of McKinley and Stoller Elementary Schools

Here we present contrasting case studies in the way principals approached conferences with teachers. Both principals were committed to the new teacher evaluation system and highly engaged. However, while Principal Andrews at Stoller was able to translate the use of the new evaluation system to have deep conversations with her teachers about instruction, Principal Ramirez at McKinley struggled to do so. The case illustrates the need for more support in the area of instructional coaching and using ratings of teaching practice to promote instructional improvement.

The principal at McKinley was highly engaged in the pilot but acknowledged her limitations in conducting conferences with teachers. Ms. Ramirez was enthusiastic about implementing the Danielson Framework. "This was exactly what I needed," she explained. "The new system and the Framework provide the guide for improving practice and the conversations about practice." She thought that it "took some time to learn to use evidence" but that, when she mastered the practice, "there was much power in the evaluation as a result." The amount of time that the process took was a concern for Ms. Ramirez, but she thought the value of the approach "far outweighed the negatives."

In her conferences, however, Ms. Ramirez relied heavily on the pre- and post-conference observation forms that the district provided to guide conference conversations. Teachers were asked to fill out the forms before meeting. In every conference, Ms. Ramirez read questions directly from the form, and she also read off the evidence from her evidence sheet and gave her ratings. As a result, the conferences consisted primarily of reading text aloud and were heavily principal-driven. Despite the scripted nature of the interactions, the principal had positive comments about the conferences, seeing them as an improvement on conversations they had using the checklist system. She recognized, however, that reading directly from her notes

was not ideal. "I imagine I will get better at this," Ms. Ramirez stated. "For now, reading makes the most sense."

The teachers at McKinley felt the principal was a good leader, but they thought the scripted nature of the conversations was stifling. When asked about Ms. Ramirez's leadership, one teacher said she could "just rave for hours" and that McKinley was "blessed to have her." Teachers were positive about the pre-conference, stating that it opened up the dialogue and allowed them the opportunity to share concerns. They saw immense potential in the new evaluation process and the use of the Danielson tool. However, McKinley teachers voiced concerns about the principal's scripted approach to the pre- and post-conference conversations. While teachers noted that this approach was systematic and fair, they felt it did not allow for deep coaching that could penetrate instructional practice.

In contrast, at Stoller, conversations between the principal and teachers were dynamic and productive—pushing teachers to ask questions, to dissect evidence of teaching practice and, at times, even to question principal ratings.

The principal at Stoller embraced the evaluation pilot and used the trust she had garnered among staff to make the Framework a cornerstone of instructional improvement at the school. Principal Andrews described her focus as "improving instruction and putting teachers on a path of reflective development." Teachers at Stoller trust the principal, and all teachers interviewed reported that Ms. Andrews was the strongest principal they had ever had (at this school or elsewhere). "She is strong on all fronts. Strong. Kind. Intuitive. Knows instruction and can articulate that," one teacher explained.

Principal Andrews was highly engaged in the implementation of the teacher evaluation initiative. She took the lead in promoting the program and garnering teacher buy-in. "If you're saying to me that you're a lifelong learner, you're reflective, you want to grow in this profession…we're going to try this tool because this is designed to help us do that." The principal continued, "It has become a part of what we do here." The teachers agreed that the Framework had taken hold at this school. Teachers attributed this to the principal's commitment. It's "part of our daily conversation," and it's something that is used throughout the year. "Regardless of whether or not CPS adopts it, she's made it hers; she'll stick with it."

The teachers at Stoller engaged in deep discussions with the principal about practice that led to improved instruction. Stoller teachers noted that the conversations were marked by "healthy debate over ratings" and "a focus on instructional improvement." In all of the pre-conferences, the principal asked the teachers to identify some components on which they would like feedback. The principal conducted her post-conferences in two parts. In the first part, the teacher

and principal reviewed the principal's evidence from the classroom observation. She provided teachers with a copy of her evidence as well as specific questions, and together they reviewed evidence that supported each component. Before the second part, the principal asked her teachers to review the evidence and rate themselves using the Danielson rubric. The principal and teacher then discussed their respective ratings for each of the components until they agreed on the final rating. Most teachers appreciated the honest look at their teaching practice.

Nearly all teachers felt that their practice had improved due to use of the Framework and most identified the conferencing process as a critical aspect of that change. Teachers reported improvement in planning, classroom management, using assessment during instruction, differentiated instruction, and student-focused learning.

Chapter 5

District Decisions in Designing a Teacher Evaluation System

Teacher evaluation will take different shapes in schools and districts across the country. In fact, even within Chicago, we found the level of implementation varied from one school to the next. This chapter is meant to serve as an implementation and design resource for districts and unions that are revitalizing teacher evaluation systems. This implementation chapter does not provide explicit answers to design questions. Instead, the goal is to draw attention to key design and logistical considerations and bring evidence from the Chicago pilot to bear on these issues, helping policymakers and practitioners to arrive at the best solutions for their own states and districts. Policymakers face a range of decisions that include, but go beyond, which observation tool to select. Many of these decisions have the potential to contribute to, or impede, successful implementation at scale.

KEY CONSIDERATIONS FOR DESIGNING TEACHER EVALUATION SYSTEMS

- **Formal Evaluation:** How do classroom observation ratings help inform a teacher's final performance evaluation rating?

- **Observation Logistics:** What is a feasible observation timeline? How many formal classroom observations of teaching practice should each teacher have in a year and who conducts the evaluations? What data systems are required to document and track evaluation observation ratings and evidence?

- **Training:** What is the most effective approach for introducing the new system to principals and teachers? What training should districts provide for principals and teachers?

- **Principal Engagement:** How should districts reach out to principals in order to engage them in teacher evaluation work? What should districts do about principals who resist the initiative?

- **Feedback for the Evaluator:** How is the evaluator held accountable for conducting the evaluation, rating fairly and accurately, and documenting the evaluation process?

For each of these topics, we provide evidence from the Chicago pilot. We also list some questions for stakeholders to consider when thinking about each of these issues.

Formal Evaluation: Feedback on Teaching Practice and Final Performance Ratings

Teacher evaluation systems can serve two primary functions: 1) provide teachers with information on their strengths and weaknesses and insights on ways to improve instruction; and 2) identify low-performing teachers, provide them with targeted support, and, in the worst cases, remove from the classroom those teachers who show no improvement. The traditional evaluation system failed to do these two important things. Both principals and teachers reported that the checklist evaluation tool did not facilitate instructional coaching, leaving teachers with little guidance about how to improve their instruction. Furthermore, historically there was little variation in performance evaluation ratings awarded to teachers—93 percent received the top two ratings of excellent and superior. As such, the evaluation system did a poor job of identifying low-performing teachers. The Danielson Framework provided more information about what happens in a teacher's classroom, both because teachers were rated in 10 different aspects of teaching and because principal ratings did not cluster at the high end of the scale.

Providing Teachers With Feedback

Classroom observations have the potential to provide a wealth of information about individual teachers. One benefit of using a rubric to evaluate teachers in multiple distinct areas of classroom practice is that principals can assess the instructional strengths and weaknesses of both individuals and groups of teachers. Principals can use this information to design and tailor professional development based on individual teacher needs and can look for school-wide trends. For example, if teachers are struggling with informal assessment, the principal may choose to identify that as a focus area for improvement. In addition, teachers receive targeted feedback on their instructional practice, and they can use that feedback to make adjustments and seek out support. In short, when used intentionally, classroom observation data can help improve instruction.

Teachers consistently receive lower ratings in the instructional aspects of teaching than in the components related to the classroom environment. Figure 7 displays the components from the Classroom Environment and Instruction domains of the Framework in order of highest rated components to lowest rated components from left to right. The order of the components is not surprising. It realistically reflects that a skill, such as Using Questioning and Discussion Techniques, is more difficult for a teacher to master than Creating an Environment of Respect and Rapport. In other words, we would expect that components in the Instruction domain are more difficult for teachers to master than those in the Classroom Environment domain.

Assigning Final Performance Evaluation Ratings

Determining the criteria for producing final evaluation ratings from classroom observation ratings is crucial for an evaluation system. With the Danielson Framework, each observation results in up to ten ratings of teaching practice. Decision makers, then, need to think about how to combine ratings from an observation tool that measures multiple components of teaching into a single performance evaluation rating. To do this, criteria need to be established using ratings on the Framework for the non-renewal, removal, or mandatory professional development for teachers and for the identification of high-performing teachers.

In this chapter, we provide historical data on teacher evaluation in Chicago. We also apply two different sets of criteria to Danielson Framework ratings of the same teachers. The comparison of these three sets of evaluation ratings illustrates the finding that the Danielson Framework did a better job of differentiating among teachers than the existing evaluation system, but it also raises questions about how to determine a teacher's final evaluation rating.

Historical Teacher Evaluation Ratings

In the past, very few teachers in Chicago were identified as "Unsatisfactory" (0.3 percent) and even fewer were removed from the classroom for inadequate performance (see Figure 8). To contrast, many businesses expect that about 10 percent of their employees are not productive in the workplace.[17] The result in Chicago is that the teacher evaluation system failed to

FIGURE 7

Teachers received higher ratings in Classroom Environment (Domain 2) than in Instruction (Domain 3)

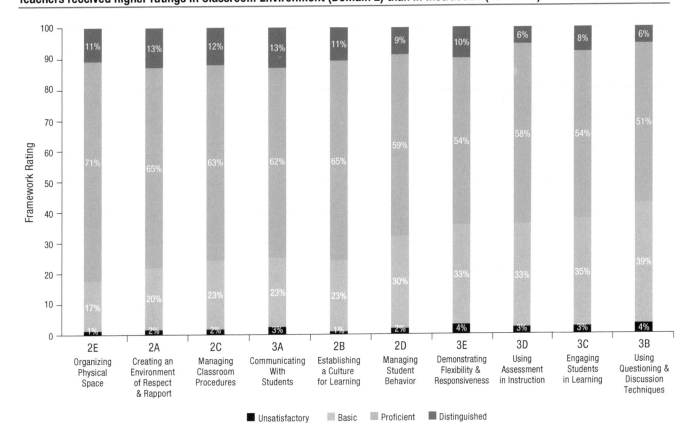

differentiate among teachers with varying skill sets. The best teachers were not rewarded or acknowledged since most teachers had the highest rating, and the lowest performing teachers were neither supported nor sanctioned.

Criteria for Translating Danielson Framework Ratings into a Final Evaluation Rating

We explore the results of applying two different sets of criteria for assigning final performance evaluation ratings using the Framework ratings. It should be noted that principals did not apply any of the criteria listed below. The district did not provide principals with official guidance on how to use the Danielson ratings to award a final performance evaluation rating; therefore, this is necessarily a hypothetical exercise. To conduct the performance evaluation rating analysis, we used principal ratings from the last observation conducted, assuming that teachers would improve over the course of the year. We restricted this analysis to the joint observation sample because this sample was randomly selected across the pilot schools, which means

that the teachers in this sample are most likely to be representative of the teaching population across CPS elementary schools. This analysis includes principal ratings of 280 teachers.

Danielson-recommended criteria (Version 1): Using the 10 Framework ratings that principals assigned per teacher, we placed each teacher into one of four performance evaluation categories:

1. At least one Unsatisfactory rating (lowest rating)

2. Mix of Basic and Proficient ratings

3. Mostly Proficient ratings

4. All Proficient and Distinguished ratings (highest rating)

Figure 9 shows the distribution of teachers across these four performance categories using principal ratings from the teacher's final observation during the school year. Principals gave 8 percent of teachers at least one Unsatisfactory rating, 34 percent of teachers a mix of Basic and Proficient ratings, 19 percent of teachers

FIGURE 8

Under the historic evaluation system, most teachers received the highest evaluation rating

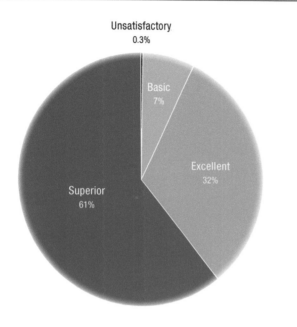

Note: The figure is based on The New Teacher Project's 2007 analysis of over 36,000 evaluation ratings assigned from 2003–06.

FIGURE 9

Using the Danielson-recommended criteria for aggregating Framework ratings, fewer teachers received the highest evaluation ratings

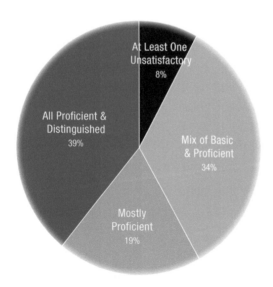

Note: The figure is based on CCSR analysis of principal ratings of 280 teachers.

mostly Proficient ratings, and 39 percent of teachers all Proficient and Distinguished ratings

Another urban district's criteria (Version 2): The second version uses another urban school district's criteria for determining a teacher's final evaluation rating.[18] These categories are much more stringent than those shown in Version 1, and there are also fewer categories of teaching performance. Using principal Framework ratings, we placed the same teachers into one of three categories:

1. **Unsatisfactory:** any Unsatisfactory rating or more than three Basic ratings

2. **Satisfactory:** mostly Proficient ratings (one, two, or three Basics)

3. **Excellent:** all Proficient ratings with at least two Distinguished ratings

Figure 10 shows the distribution of the *same sample of teachers* across the three categories. Using the more stringent criteria, 33 percent of the teachers in this

FIGURE 10

Using the same ratings data but applying another urban district's criteria for aggregating Framework ratings, just one-quarter of teachers would receive the highest evaluation rating into one final evaluation rating

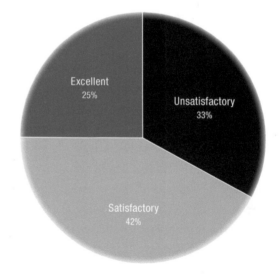

Note: The figure is based on CCSR analysis of principal ratings of 280 teachers.

sample would sort into the Unsatisfactory category, 42 percent would be given a satisfactory rating, and only 25 percent would have a final rating of excellent.

Applying different criteria for final evaluation changes the distribution of teacher performance ratings. The two different versions of criteria for aggregating Framework ratings into a final evaluation rating tell two very different stories. Looking at Version 1, 39 percent of teachers would sort into the highest category. But in Version 2, only 25 percent would be in the highest category. Thus, different criteria for aggregating Framework ratings from the very same lesson will result in very different distributions of teacher evaluation ratings. Regardless of the criteria applied, both sets of criteria do a better job of differentiating among teachers than the checklist system did.

QUESTIONS TO CONSIDER

- How will districts set the benchmarks for final performance evaluation ratings?

- Other than classroom observation, what measures of teaching practice will districts use to characterize teacher performance?

- How will districts align various components of human capital systems: teacher evaluation systems, hiring and recruiting teachers, professional development, and teacher remediation and removal?

Observation Choices and Logistics

The observation of teaching practice is at the center of teacher evaluation. District leaders face a number of decisions about classroom observations. Some principals claimed that they get a more accurate representation of teaching when they "pop in" to classrooms unannounced, so districts might want to think about the role of principal pop-in observations in formal evaluation. Another consideration is the timeline for conducting formal evaluations—how often should a teacher be formally evaluated, and are there different requirements for newer and more veteran teachers? We describe issues that emerged with conducting classroom observations, including how ratings changed when teachers were not aware that an observation was going to happen and what we learned from principals and teachers about challenges with scheduling observations.

Scheduled Versus Unscheduled Observations

As part of the pilot evaluation system in Chicago, principals scheduled observations with their teachers in advance. In part this was necessitated by the addition of a pre-conference, in which the specific lesson the principal would observe was discussed. However, conversations with principals revealed that, in the past, some principals included one or more pop-in observations as a part of the formal evaluation process. A pop-in observation is unplanned, so the teacher does not know the principal will observe. A few principals relied primarily on pop-in observations.

Principals expressed two concerns about the requirement that observations were scheduled in advance. First, scheduled visits were difficult because of the complexity of the daily lives of principals. Second, principals felt that scheduled observations did not necessarily capture the teaching that happens day in and day out. One principal stated, "Those drive-by, those pop-in visits give you a truer, more authentic sense of what's going on in that classroom than when you announce yourself." Many principals that we interviewed said that classrooms look different when they pop in. They worried that the types of teachers who put on the "dog and pony show" might only listen to feedback from the formal observation and brush off any feedback given after a pop-in observation. They suggested that a combination of scheduled and unscheduled observations would allow for a more representative picture of a teacher's actual level of performance.

For observations in which both the principal and the external observer were present, teachers were informed in advance of their scheduled observation.[19] While external observers were in schools conducting the formal observations with principals, they also visited other teachers' classrooms unannounced. We compared the observers' ratings in Year 2 from the formal joint observations to the informal pop-in observations to see if, as some principals said, classroom practice was rated at a lower level when teachers did not know there would be an observation.

FIGURE 11

Teacher ratings were lower in unscheduled observations in five of the ten Framework components

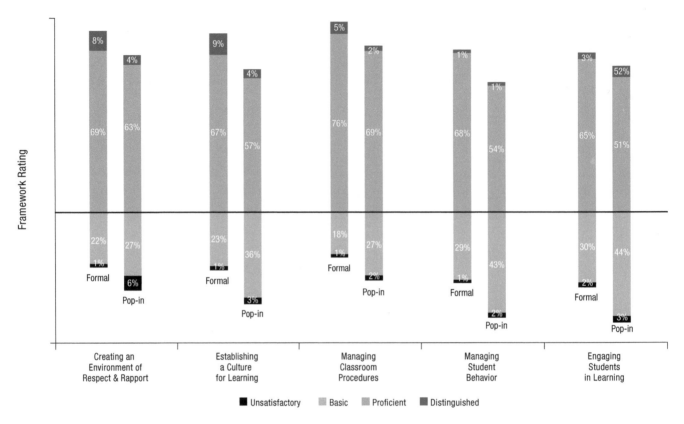

Legend: ■ Unsatisfactory ▧ Basic ▨ Proficient ▧ Distinguished

Note: Data used in this figure consist of external observer ratings from 404 formal observations and 222 pop-in observations in the second year of the pilot. Ratings in the other five Danielson Framework components were not significantly different in pop-in observations than in scheduled observations.

Indeed, external observers' ratings were lower, on average, in unscheduled than in scheduled observations for five of the ten Framework components (see Figure 11). Of the five components, four were in the Classroom Environment domain. The fact that ratings were lower in pop-in observations supports the principals' claim that scheduled observations may not reflect a teacher's job performance on a daily basis.

It is noteworthy that the majority of the components that were significantly lower in pop-in observations are in the Classroom Environment domain rather than the domain focused on Instruction. Ratings on almost all instructional components, however, did not vary based on whether the observations were scheduled or unscheduled. This finding suggests that the extra care that teachers put into lesson planning for a scheduled observation may result in better management, but not necessarily better instruction. The one exception is with the Engaging Students in Learning component

(3C). Student engagement was one of the lowest rated components (principals and observers rated this component as Unsatisfactory or Basic in 38 percent of the joint observations as shown in Figure 7). This finding suggests that more careful lesson planning and conferencing about a lesson has the potential to result in activities and assignments that are more engaging to students.

Observation Timeline

Multiple observations across a year provide a teacher with the opportunity to demonstrate his/her skills, ensuring that a teacher is not punished for having a "bad day" and allowing a teacher to demonstrate improvement across a year. However, principals' schedules are constrained; their limited time must also be considered because evaluating teachers in a meaningful way is time consuming. District leaders must make decisions about two aspects concerning the

Chicago Teacher Evaluation Timeframe

- Non-tenured teachers: annually

- Low-rated tenured teachers: annually

- High-rated tenured teachers: every other year

timing of observations, balancing the desire for high quality feedback on teaching practice and principals' time constraints. First, how many observations of teaching practice are enough to make an evaluative judgment? Second, how often should teachers receive formal evaluation ratings?

Urban principals have a lot on their plates—they're expected to be the chief education officer and the chief operation officer in their building. While most principals describe their main role as instructional leader, they get pulled in other directions and do not spend as much time in classrooms as they would like. Finding the time to engage in the conference process— preparing, scheduling, and holding the conferences themselves—was difficult for most principals.

Principals in Chicago evaluate all teachers in the building every other year. Typically, one observation occurs in the fall and the other occurs in the spring. Given the labor-intensive nature of the evidence-based teacher evaluation process, many Chicago principals were concerned that they might not be able to manage two observations per year for their entire staff. Both principals and teachers had difficulties scheduling observations. Principals reported that observations were frequently canceled due to emergencies in the school, principals being summoned to attend last-minute meetings at the area or central office, and teacher absences. Some teachers expressed frustration at the time expended on making detailed lesson plans, meeting with the principal before the observation, and then having to reschedule the observation and do the extensive planning all over again for another lesson. Talking about difficulties with scheduling, one teacher said of his principal, "The hard part is fitting in the post-conference, even the pre-[conference], because

[the principal] gets so over-occupied doing other things. So you think he's coming at this time on this day, and then it might not happen."

Multiply this scheduling challenge across the entire teaching staff in a school, and it is no surprise that many principals felt that observing all their teachers in one year would be nearly impossible–especially for principals with a larger staff. One principal stated, "The logistics around scheduling all the pieces of the observation feels like a daunting task, even if the payoff is worth it."

Other districts have developed ways to alleviate time pressures. Some districts have utilized a staggered evaluation schedule. Others have expanded the pool of observers to include teacher leaders, colleagues, or external experts.

Tracking Observation Data

Observations that result in multiple ratings, such as the component ratings on the Danielson Framework, provide a more detailed description of instruction than what is provided using traditional evaluation tools. These detailed data can be used for a variety of purposes—to monitor ratings of individual teachers and schools, to determine professional development needs across the system, and to look for evidence of improvements in teacher quality over time. Design of a data system must not only take into account these varied purposes but also consider usability for principals and other evaluators.

Program administrators in Chicago integrated a ratings database into a website called DS2, which principals were already using to manage other personnel information. From the beginning of the pilot, the principals reported that the data entry piece of the evaluation system was overwhelming and time consuming. Most cited it as the biggest challenge of the evaluation pilot. As time passed, principals continued to struggle with issues related to time and data entry in DS2. One principal reported, "I was trained to do my observations on paper.... I have all the documentation and forms in my accountability binder, but I haven't gotten to DS2. I understand the importance of that for tracking things and making things easier in the long run, but getting to it initially has been a challenge."

Most of the administrators' criticisms related to two issues. Some principals were overwhelmed by the whole process of capturing evidence in the classroom, coding that evidence, entering the evidence in DS2, and assigning the rating. Many principals preferred to hand write their observation notes during their observations; being required to type their notes to enter them into the DS2 system added another step to the data entry process.

QUESTIONS TO CONSIDER

- How many observations of teaching practice are required to measure performance fairly and adequately?

- What is the appropriate combination of formal/scheduled observations and informal/pop-in observations?

- How often should teachers be formally evaluated? Is the evaluation schedule different for newer teachers than it is for veteran teachers?

- Given the time constraints, what can districts do to alleviate the evaluation burden of principals in order to make teacher evaluation a priority?

- What is the best way to collect observation data systematically?

Training for Principals and Teachers

The introduction of the Excellence in Teaching Pilot marked a significant change in teacher evaluation. Communicating and messaging around the new system is one potential way to help practitioners shift from the old evaluation system to the new evaluation system. One key arena for district staff to communicate with stakeholders was through the training sessions for principals and teachers. We describe the training—the content, the timeframe, and the structure—as well as what we learned from principals and teachers about what worked and what didn't.

District-Provided Training for Principals

Principals received three different types of training, as well as optional support from district staff.[20] The district provided one three-day summer training, four half-day professional development sessions throughout the year, and regular meetings with fellow principals to discuss the evaluation process that took the form of professional learning communities (PLCs).

Principals received extensive training, and they liked it. We estimate that principals received about fifty hours of training in their first year of implementation. Principals were generally positive about the training they received and reported that this intensive, ongoing support influenced their ability to implement the new system. According to one principal, the initial training helped provide "a fresh perspective and a new standard to look at classroom observation. While we had always taken some type of notes when we went in to do classroom observations, there was never the dialogue piece and the guided language to keep the conversation open with the teacher you're observing and really focusing on the idea of improving instruction."

Principals especially appreciated the professional learning communities that allowed them to work in small groups with other administrators and talk about classroom observation data from their own schools. Principals appreciated the collaborative time: "When you get to talk to colleagues and get some of their direct feedback, I think that's always reaffirming. It tends to break down a lot of barriers that you may go into a new project with."

However, principals noted substantial demands on their time to attend training. There was a consensus that lack of time was not unique to this pilot. One principal said, "…You're always feeling like you're being pulled away. I don't think that's a reflection on the pilot per se. I just think it's the nature of the job and the multi-tasking that we have to do." It should be noted that in some cases principals who were initially reluctant to spend much time in training later acknowledged that the training gave them the opportunity to collaborate with their peers.

Principals wanted more support in areas related to instructional leadership. Most of the principal training was focused on how to use the Framework. The goal was to familiarize principals with the different pieces of the Framework, how to collect evidence in a classroom observation, and how to evaluate the level of teaching in the observation. Little time was spent on the other pieces of the evaluation system. Principals reported that they needed help in these areas:

- How to have honest, reflective conversations with teachers about their practice

- How to use the Framework data to guide professional development decisions

- How to have difficult conversations with teachers who are under-performing

- How to talk to teachers about the new system and the impetus for replacing the checklist

- How to schedule observations, as well as pre- and post-conferences, with the teaching staff

Principals' reports on the type of support they needed during training coincide with the findings presented in Chapter 4. Many principals struggled to provide the type of feedback that would help improve instruction, and principals acknowledged this weakness and asked for more support in these areas.

QUESTIONS TO CONSIDER

- How much support do principals need?

- Who provides training and support for principals? Who are the experts in the evaluation system?

- What kinds of support do principals need? How much training should districts offer around using the observation tool to rate teaching practice? How much training should districts offer around using the observation tool to guide instructional coaching conversations?

- What will be the mechanism for answering ongoing questions and providing support for teachers?

District-Provided Training for Teachers

Training and support for teachers was more limited than that for principals.[21] Teachers received two school-based professional development sessions that provided an overview of the Charlotte Danielson Framework, totaling about three hours of support.

Teacher understanding of the evaluation system was limited. Compared with principals, teachers received less training and less direct information about the new initiative. Teachers participating in the pilot schools received training on the Danielson Framework at the beginning of the year during in-service days. Perhaps because the initial sessions were scheduled at such a busy time of the year right before the beginning of school, these half-day training sessions did not facilitate teacher buy-in. Many teachers said they did not remember the training; those who did, tended to find it only moderately useful. One teacher said, "I was thinking about setting up my room, not this. By the time I was observed, it seemed like a million years since the overview."

Most principals noted that their teachers have a very poor understanding of the Framework and that their teachers could benefit from more extensive training. When we talked to teachers in the first year of the pilot, many of them (65 percent) were positive about the training; however nearly a quarter (23 percent) did not remember the training at all. This problem worsened in the second year of the pilot—in almost all case study schools, teachers struggled to talk about the training in any detailed way (if they even remembered the training).

Ultimately teachers reported feeling removed from communication and training. As a result, their access to the initiative, the depth of their understanding of the Framework, and their buy-in and engagement depended on the translation of the principal. One teacher described her confusion about the purpose of the pilot and her desire for more information: "I need to find more in-depth information about the Danielson [Framework] because it wasn't clear. I didn't even know we were gonna do that. I didn't know it was part of the observation."

Lack of teacher knowledge can create mistrust between teachers and the principal and be a barrier to implementation. The district message to teachers around the pilot system was that the Framework would be used for professional development and feedback, while the checklist would still be the source of their final evaluation rating. However, many teachers said they did not understand how they would be evaluated, which was a shortcoming in the implementation process.

Due to lack of information, some teachers even thought they were being targeted. One teacher said, "I thought I was chosen because I was a bad teacher. I thought the observer was from [central office], valuating whether I should get fired." For teachers, evaluations are personal and can be very stressful. Confusion about the purpose of the pilot system caused unnecessary mistrust in some schools, which made the pilot more difficult to implement. One principal described a strong atmosphere of suspicion in her school, especially among weaker teachers. About these teachers, she said, "Many times your [struggling] teachers are very, very union savvy. They're almost like lawyers when it comes to that union book, so if you do not dot every 'i' and cross every 't,' then you can have a grievance." While the district hoped this program would help teachers improve, teachers in some schools were confused about the purpose and assumed the worst.

QUESTIONS TO CONSIDER

- How will the district communicate with all teachers? Should all communication with teachers flow through the principal? How can the district and union work together to reach out to teachers?

- What is the message that teachers should receive about the goals of teacher evaluation?

- What will be the mechanism for answering ongoing questions and providing support for teachers?

Engaging Principals in Teacher Evaluation

In many ways, principals are the gatekeepers of the teacher evaluation system. As the system was implemented in Chicago, principals were the main source of information and messaging for teachers, and in this way they had the potential to shape teacher attitudes and potentially garner teacher buy-in. As has historically been the case in Chicago, principals were also the main evaluators of teacher practice.[22] They made the final call on a teacher's evaluation rating and whether or not a non-tenured teacher should return to the school the next year. Principals were also the instructional leaders in their buildings. They held conferences with teachers about instructional practice, defined instructional priorities for the school, and organized professional development for staff. Because principals control all these aspects of teacher evaluation,

the engagement and buy-in of principals is critical to successful implementation of any reform or initiative.

Based on 39 interviews, we were able to characterize principal engagement, ranging from those who were highly engaged in the work to those who were skeptical and even resisted the pilot initiative:

- **High Engagement (57 percent):** These principals were highly engaged in all aspects of the evaluation process, including training, conferencing, and observing teachers. A small subgroup of these principals was identified as having made a paradigm shift in their conception of teacher evaluation, acknowledging that they had been subjective in their past evaluations.

- **Mixed Emotions (28 percent):** These principals were positive about some aspects of the evaluation system, but they were critical of other aspects. Most of these principals were overwhelmed by multiple district and area initiatives and saw this program as "just another thing to do."

- **Resistant (15 percent):** These principals were mostly negative about the evaluation system. Many principals in this group felt they were already adequately evaluating their teachers and that the new system did not add anything new.

Most principals were highly engaged with the new system. These **high-engagement** principals had positive attitudes about the Danielson Framework and the conferencing process, and they also reported high teacher buy-in at their schools. Further, these principals attributed improvements and changes in instructional practice to use of the evaluation system. These changes occurred in the ways that teachers grouped students, assessed student learning, and planned lessons.

A small group (six principals or 27 percent of the high-engagement principals) made a "paradigm shift" as a result of their participation in the pilot. These principals talked about how their past evaluations had been subjective or how they had misidentified teacher strengths or weaknesses when they did not have an observation rubric. The Danielson Framework, as well as the pre- and post-conference conversations, led them to see evaluation and their teachers' performance differently.

Principals with **mixed emotions** about the pilot system tended to be negative—less about the pilot itself but about how the district initiatives piled up. They saw the pilot as an additional initiative, layered on top of countless existing programs that were already in their schools, leaving little time for the labor-intensive evaluation approach. Despite being overwhelmed, these principals still noted changes in teacher practice due to participation in the evaluation system. Whereas the high-engagement principals noted changes in instruction, the mixed-emotions principals saw benefits in increased compliance and planning. Principals were enthusiastic that the new system brought teachers better prepared to conferences and that teachers followed the lesson plans they submitted—these principals felt the new evaluation system created a greater sense of accountability for teachers in terms of lesson planning and following through on suggestions discussed during conferences.

Resistant principals were mostly negative about the Framework and conferences, stating that they were already doing a good job with teacher evaluation or that they "just knew" teachers' abilities. These principals perceived that the evaluation system had no impact on instructional practice and described their teachers' buy-in as low to medium. They also placed teacher evaluation at the low end of priorities compared with their other responsibilities.

QUESTIONS TO CONSIDER

- How will districts engage principals around teacher evaluation, given that principals are often the gatekeepers of this work?

- What should districts do about principals who are very resistant to the work? How will districts identify these principals?

- What efforts will districts make to help principals shift from weak teacher evaluation practices to more rigorous ways of looking at teaching practice?

Holding Evaluators Accountable

Districts need to think about accountability—how to hold evaluators accountable for rating fairly and accurately. In Chicago, we found that most principals were rating teaching practice reliably, and both teachers and principals said the pilot process was less subjective than the checklist system. These findings raise questions about the best way to hold evaluators accountable for rating practice accurately and using classroom observation evidence in evaluation. We provide some ways in which principals in Chicago were held accountable, as well as sources of feedback that they received.

Sources of Accountability and Feedback

In Chicago, one unintended source of accountability was the joint observation with the external observer. District staff worked with principals to schedule the joint observations, and principals cited this as an extra layer of accountability—one that they appreciated. Some principals said the joint observations kept them on track with scheduling and conducting classroom observations in their school. This is also further evidence that some principals need additional support with maintaining an observation schedule, as mentioned previously.

Another source of accountability came from the study. After conducting the observation, principals had to enter ratings into an electronic database integrated in a district website. Study researchers monitored the ratings entered by principals weekly. If a principal did not enter ratings data within a week of an observation, study researchers would inform district pilot administrators who would then individually contact principals via email reminding them to enter their ratings data. Most principals complied after one or two reminders.

Principals also received feedback about their ratings from the research team and the district, which incentivized them to complete their scheduled observations and enter ratings. In Year 1 of the pilot (2008–09), if principals completed and entered ratings and evidence for four of their scheduled observations, researchers provided a ratings report detailing their ratings in comparison with observer ratings. In Year 2 of the pilot (2009–10), the district also provided reports to principals about how their ratings compared to observer ratings.

In Year 2, all pilot school administrators received a mid-year fidelity of implementation report from the district detailing the following:

- Administrator participation in pilot training

- The percent of observations completed

- A severity index telling principals and assistant principals whether they were considered too lenient, lenient, within range, severe, or too severe in comparison with external observer ratings

Principals were positive about the feedback they received on their ratings. They stated that they wanted more feedback and wished they could compare their ratings to external observer's ratings right away, suggesting that using a feedback mechanism might serve as a good a source of accountability for other districts. This might include hiring external observers to conduct observations with principals at time points throughout the year or analyzing ratings to identify principals with extremes in their ratings for support and training.

QUESTIONS TO CONSIDER

- What feedback will principals, or other evaluators, receive about their ratings, especially when they are first implementing a new teacher evaluation system?

- How will districts monitor teacher ratings to ensure that principals are rating teachers accurately over time?

- Will there be a certification process for principals and other evaluators?

Conclusion

Our study of the Excellence in Teaching Pilot in Chicago reveals some positive outcomes: the observation tool was demonstrated to be reliable and valid. Principals and teachers reported they had more meaningful conversations about instruction. The majority of principals in the pilot were engaged and positive about their participation. At the same time, our study identifies areas of concern: principals were more likely to use the Distinguished rating. Our interviews with principals confirm that principals intentionally boost their ratings to the highest category to preserve relationships. And, while principals and teachers reported having better conversations than they had in the past, there are indications that both principals and teachers still have much to learn about how to translate a rating on an instructional rubric into deep conversation that drives improvement in the classroom. Future work in teacher evaluation must attend to these critical areas of success, as well as these areas of concern, in order to build effective teacher evaluation systems.

Though practitioners and policymakers rightly spend a good deal of time comparing the effectiveness of one rubric over another, a fair and meaningful evaluation hinges on far more than the merits of a particular tool. An observation rubric is simply a tool, one which can be used effectively or ineffectively. Reliability and validity are functions of the *users of the tool*, as well as of the tool itself. The quality of implementation depends on principal and observer buy-in and capacity, as well as the depth and quality of training and support they receive.

Similarly, an observation tool cannot promote instructional improvement in isolation. A rigorous instructional rubric plays a critical role in defining effective instruction and creating a shared language for teachers and principals to talk about instruction, but it is the conversations themselves that act as the true lever for instructional improvement and teacher development. Our analysis suggests that principals and teachers need training and support to learn how to have meaningful conversations about improving instructional practice.

At the same time, successfully implementing these new systems requires a shift in the way principals and teachers think about teacher evaluation. Evidence-based evaluation requires principals to devote a significant amount of time and energy to conducting, analyzing, and discussing observations of instructional practice. The success is dependent upon principals valuing this practice enough to devote such time and energy. For some principals, it will require a shift away from the idea that they "just know" good practice when they see it, to seeing teacher evaluation as a process of collecting information to deeply diagnose teachers' strengths and weaknesses to improve instruction.

The shift to evidence-based teacher evaluation similarly requires teachers to conceptualize their instructional practice as constantly evolving, open to scrutiny, and in need of tweaking and improvement. It challenges norms in the teaching profession of the privatized practice that is so common in schools.[23]

In short, building a successful evidence-based teacher evaluation system requires an intentional, long-term commitment. It begins with the selection of a strong instructional rubric to promote shared language and values about instructional improvement. It is situated within a well-conceived, carefully articulated system that details the number of observations, who will conduct observations, the timing and structure of conferences, and the stakes of the system. Most importantly, a successful evidence-based teacher evaluation system must ensure that these tools, ratings, and systems are supported by professional development that help principals and teachers to re-conceptualize teacher evaluation as a process intended to promote and support teacher development and as a vehicle to improve instructional practice.

References

Baker, Eva L., Paul E. Barton, Linda Darling-Hammond, Edward Haertel, Helen F. Ladd, Robert L. Linn, Diane Ravitch, Richard Rothstein, Richard J. Shavelson, and Lorrie A. Shepard (2010)
Problems With the Use of Student Test Scores to Evaluate Teachers. Washington, D.C.: Economic Policy Institute.

Costa, Arthur L., and Robert J. Garmston (2002)
Cognitive Coaching: A Foundation for Renaissance Schools. Norwood, MA: Christopher-Gordon Publishers, Inc.

Danielson, Charlotte (2007)
Enhancing Professional Practice: A Framework for Teaching (2nd ed.). Alexandria, VA: Association for Supervision and Curriculum Development.

Darling-Hammond, Linda (1996)
What Matters Most: A Competent Teacher for Every Child. *Phi Delta Kappan.* 78(3): 193-200.

Eisner, Elliot W. (1992)
Education Reform and the Ecology of Schooling. *Teachers College Record.* 93(4): 610-627.

Haefele, Donald L. (1993)
Evaluating Teachers: A Call for Change. *Journal of Personnel Evaluation in Education.* 7(1): 21-31.

Lortie, Daniel C. (2002)
Schoolteacher: A Sociological Study (2nd ed.). Chicago: University of Chicago Press.

McLaughlin, Milbrey W. (1990)
Embracing Contraries: Implementing and Sustaining Teacher Evaluation. In *The New Handbook of Teacher Evaluation*, eds. J. Millman and L. Darling-Hammond. Newbury Park, CA: Sage.

The New Teacher Project (2007)
Teacher Hiring, Assignment, and Transfer in Chicago Public Schools. Brooklyn, NY: The New Teacher Project.

Performance Evaluation Reform Act (2010)
Law of Illinois, 2010. Illinois Public Act 096-0861.

Searfross, Lyndon W. and Billie J. Enz (1996)
Can Teacher Evaluation Reflect Holistic Instruction? *Education Leadership.* 53(6): 38-41.

Small Newspaper Group (2005)
The Hidden Costs of Tenure Series. http://the hiddencostsoftenure.com.

Tyler, John H., Eric S. Taylor, Thomas J. Kane, and Amy L. Wooten (2010)
Using Student Performance Data to Identify Effective Classroom Practices. *American Economic Review.* 100(2): 256–60.

U.S. Department of Education (2009)
Resources for Race to the Top. http://www2.ed.gov/programs/racetothetop/index.html.

Van Sciver, James H. (1990)
Teacher Dismissals. *Phi Delta Kappan.* 72(4): 318-319.

Wise, Arthur E., Linda Darling-Hammond, Milbrey W. McLaughlin, and Harriet T. Bernstein (1984)
Teacher Evaluation: A Study of Effective Practices. Santa Monica, CA: Rand.

Appendix A: Charlotte Danielson Framework for Teaching Modified for Use in Chicago Public Schools

Domain 2: The Classroom Environment

Component	Unsatisfactory	Basic
2A: Creating An Environment of Respect and Rapport	Classroom interactions, both between the teacher and students and among students, are negative, inappropriate, or insensitive to students' cultural backgrounds, and characterized by sarcasm, put-downs, or conflict.	Classroom interactions, both between the teacher and students and among students, are generally appropriate and free from conflict but may be characterized by occasional displays of insensitivity or lack of responsiveness to cultural or developmental differences among students.
2B: Establishing a Culture for Learning	The classroom environment conveys a negative culture for learning, characterized by low teacher commitment to the subject, low expectations for student achievement, little respect for or knowledge of students' diverse cultures and little or no student pride in work.	Teacher's attempt to create a culture for learning are partially successful, with little teacher commitment to the subject, modest expectations for student achievement, some respect for or knowledge of students' diverse cultures and little student pride in work.
2C: Managing Classroom Procedures	Much instructional time is lost due to inefficient classroom routines and procedures, for transitions, handling of supplies, and performance of non-instructional duties.	Some instructional time is lost due to only partially effective classroom routines and procedures, for transitions, handling of supplies, and performance of non-instructional duties.
2D: Managing Student Behavior	There is no evidence that standards of conduct have been established, and little or no teacher monitoring of student behavior. Response to student misbehavior is repressive, or disrespectful of student dignity.	The teacher has made an effort to establish standards of conduct for students. Teacher tries, with uneven results, to monitor student behavior and respond to student misbehavior.
2E: Organizing Physical Space	Teacher makes poor use of the physical environment, resulting in unsafe or inaccessible conditions for some students or a significant mismatch between the physical arrangement and the lesson activities.	Teacher's classroom is safe, and essential learning is accessible to most students, but the physical arrangement only partially supports the learning activities. Teacher's use of physical resources, including computer technology, is moderately effective.

Proficient	Distinguished
Classroom interactions, between teacher and students and among students, are polite and respectful, reflecting general warmth and caring, and are appropriate to the cultural and developmental differences among groups of students.	Classroom interactions among the teacher and individual students are highly respectful, reflecting genuine warmth and caring and sensitivity to students' cultures and levels of development. Students themselves ensure high levels of civility among members of the class.
The classroom culture is characterized by high expectations for most students, genuine commitment to the subject by both teacher and students, respect for and knowledge of students' diverse cultures, with students demonstrating pride in their work.	High levels of student engagement and teacher passion for the subject create a culture for learning in which everyone shares a belief in the importance of the subject, and all students hold themselves to high standards of performance, for example by initiating improvements to their work. Teacher and students demonstrate high levels of respect for and knowledge of diverse student cultures.
Little instructional time is lost due to classroom routines and procedures, for transitions, handling of supplies, and performance of non-instructional duties, which occur smoothly.	Students contribute to the seamless operation of classroom routines and procedures, for transitions, handling of supplies, and performance of non-instructional duties.
Standards of conduct are clear to students, and the teacher monitors student behavior against those standards. Teacher response to student misbehavior is appropriate and respects the students' dignity.	Standards of conduct are clear, with evidence of student participation in setting them. Teacher's monitoring of student behavior is subtle and preventive, and teacher's response to student misbehavior is sensitive to individual student needs. Students take an active role in monitoring the standards of behavior.
Teacher's classroom is safe, and learning is accessible to all students; teacher ensures that the physical arrangement supports the learning activities, (when applicable) Teacher makes effective use of physical resources, including computer technology.	The classroom is safe, and the physical environment ensures the learning of all students, including those with special needs. Students contribute to the use or adaptation of the physical environment to advance learning. Technology is used skillfully, as appropriate to the lesson.

Domain 3: Instruction

Component	Unsatisfactory	Basic
3A: Communicating With Students	Expectations for learning, directions and procedures, and explanations of content are unclear or confusing to students. Teacher's use of language contains errors or is inappropriate to students' diverse cultures or levels of development.	Expectations for learning, directions and procedures, and explanations of content are clarified after initial confusion; teacher's use of language is correct but may not be completely appropriate to students' diverse cultures or levels of development.
3B: Using Questioning and Discussion Techniques	Teacher's questions are low-level or inappropriate, eliciting limited student participation, and recitation rather than discussion.	Some of the teacher's questions elicit a thoughtful response, but most are low-level, posed in rapid succession. Teachers' attempts to engage all students in the discussion are only partially successful.
3C: Engaging Students in Learning	Activities and assignments, materials, and groupings of students are inappropriate to the instructional outcomes, or levels of understanding, resulting in little intellectual engagement. The lesson has no structure or is poorly paced.	Activities and assignments, materials, and groupings of students are partially appropriate to the instructional outcomes, or levels of understanding, resulting in moderate intellectual engagement. The lesson has a recognizable structure but is not fully maintained.
	Activities, assignments, and materials are not appropriate for diverse cultures.	Activities, assignments, and materials are partially appropriate for diverse cultures.
3D: Using Assessment in Instruction*	Assessment is not used in instruction, either through students' awareness of the assessment criteria, monitoring of progress by teacher or students, or through feedback to students.	Assessment is occasionally used in instruction, through some monitoring of progress of learning by teacher and/or students. Feedback to students is uneven, and students are aware of only some of the assessment criteria used to evaluate their work.
3E: Demonstrating Flexibility and Responsiveness	Teacher adheres to the instruction plan in spite of evidence of poor student understanding or of students' lack of interest, and fails to respond to student questions; teacher assumes no responsibility for students' failure to understand.	Teacher demonstrates moderate flexibility and responsiveness to student questions, needs and interests during a lesson, and seeks to ensure the success of all students.

Proficient	Distinguished
Expectations for learning, directions and procedures, and explanations of content are clear to students. Communications are appropriate to students' diverse cultures and levels of development	Expectations for learning, directions and procedures, and explanations of content are clear to students. Teacher's oral and written communication is clear and expressive, appropriate to students' diverse cultures and levels of development, and anticipates possible student misconceptions.
Most of the teacher's questions elicit a thoughtful response, and the teacher allows sufficient time for students to answer. All students participate in the discussion, with the teacher stepping aside when appropriate.	Questions reflect high expectations and are culturally and developmentally appropriate. Students formulate many of the high-level questions and ensure that all voices are heard.
Activities and assignments, materials, and groupings of students are fully appropriate to the instructional outcomes, and students' cultures and levels of understanding. All students are engaged in work of a high level of rigor. The lesson's structure is coherent, with appropriate pace.	Students are highly intellectually engaged throughout the lesson in higher order learning, and make material contributions to the activities, student groupings, and materials. The lesson is adapted as needed to the needs of individuals, and the structure and pacing allow for student reflection and closure.
Activities, assignments, and materials are fully appropriate for diverse cultures.	Students assist in ensuring that activities, assignments and materials are fully appropriate for diverse cultures.
Assessment is regularly used in instruction, through self-assessment by students, monitoring of progress of learning by teacher and/or students, and through high quality feedback to students. Students are fully aware of the assessment criteria used to evaluate their work.	Multiple assessments are used in instruction, through student involvement in establishing the assessment criteria, self-assessment by students and monitoring of progress by both students and teachers, and high quality feedback to students from a variety of sources.
Teacher ensures the successful learning of all students, making adjustments as needed to instruction plans and responding to student questions, needs and interests.	Teacher is highly responsive to individual students' needs, interests and questions, making even major lesson adjustments as necessary to meet instructional goals, and persists in ensuring the success of all students.

Appendix B:
Chicago Public Schools Evaluation Checklist

CLASSROOM TEACHER VISITATION

This form is **required**. It should be used in conjunction with the "Post-Observation Framework Feedback Form" (Form 5B).

Teacher's Name: _____ Room_____ Date _____

_____ School_____ Subject/Grade_____

(Place a (✓) or brief comment in the appropriate column.)

	Strength	Weakness	Does Not Apply
I. Instruction			
a) Provides written lesson plans and preparation in accordance with the objectives of the instructional program.	_____	_____	_____
b) Establishes positive learning expectation standards for all students.	_____	_____	_____
c) Periodically evaluates pupils' progress and keeps up-to-date records of pupils' achievements.	_____	_____	_____
d) Applies contemporary principles of learning theory and teaching methodology.	_____	_____	_____
e) Draws from the range of instruction materials available in the school.	_____	_____	_____
f) Exhibits willingness to participate in the development and implementation of new ideas and teaching techniques.	_____	_____	_____
g) Provides bulletin board and interest areas reflective of current student work.	_____	_____	_____
h) Exhibits and applies knowledge of the curriculum content related to subject area and instructional level.	_____	_____	_____
i) Shows evidence of student performance and progress.	_____	_____	_____
II. School Environment			
a) Establishes and maintains reasonable rules of conduct within the classroom consistent with the provisions of the Student Code of Conduct.	_____	_____	_____
b) Maintains attendance books, lesson plan, seating chart(s), and grade book accurately.	_____	_____	_____
c) Uses recommendations and suggestions from conference and special education staffings.	_____	_____	_____
d) Encourages student growth in self discipline and positive self-concept.	_____	_____	_____
e) Makes students aware of the teacher's objectives and expectations.	_____	_____	_____
f) Practices fairness in teacher-pupil relationships.	_____	_____	_____
g) Exhibits an understanding and respect for students as individuals.	_____	_____	_____
III. Professional and Personal Standards			
a) Presents an appearance that does not adversely affect the students' ability to learn.	_____	_____	_____
b) Demonstrates proper diction and grammatical usage when addressing students.	_____	_____	_____
c) Uses sound and professional judgment.	_____	_____	_____

IV. Local School Unit Criteria

a) CPS Framework for Teaching and related process

b) _____

c) _____

Comments: _____

_____

Appendix C:
Danielson Framework Training for Pilot Principals and Teachers

Tables A1 and A2 provide information about the content and timeframe of the principal and teacher training in the first year of pilot implementation.

TABLE A1

Principal Training

Principal Training	When	What
Summer Institute	Three days in the summer prior to implementation	Initial overview of the pilot system and the Danielson Framework. Principals attended with their assistant principal and 1–2 teacher leaders of their choosing.
		Day 1: Framework Domain 2 (Classroom Environment) and the levels of performance (Unsatisfactory, Basic, Proficient, Distinguished). Principals watched a video of a lesson and rated it in Domain 2.
		Day 2: Framework Domain 3 (Instruction), as well as Domains 1 (Planning and Preparation) and 4 (Professional Responsibilities). The afternoon was devoted to cognitive coaching strategies.
		Day 3: Logistics of implementation, including observation and conference requirements, guidelines for gathering evidence and entering data, how the pilot aligns with district goals, and information about the CCSR study.
Half-Day Refreshers	Four times throughout the school year	**Session 1 (October):** Strategies for time management in response to principal concerns about observation scheduling and documentation. Principals also watched a video of a lesson, wrote down evidence, and assigned Danielson levels of performance.
		Session 2 (November): Charlotte Danielson spoke at this session. She provided a lot of specific guidance in response to principal concerns. CCSR also shared early results from the classroom observation data, looking at principal ratings and observer ratings.
		Session 3 (February): This session was the last session before principals gave non-tenured teachers final evaluation ratings for the year, so trainers offered guidance in this area. Each principal received a detailed report from CCSR showing how their ratings compared to the observer ratings, and half of the session was devoted to analyzing these reports. Principals also watched a video of a lesson, wrote down evidence, and assigned Danielson levels of performance.
		Session 4 (March): A wrap-up session in which principals brainstormed effective ways to improve teaching practice by planning school-level professional development on components that were tough for teachers to master. They reviewed gathering evidence for Domains 1 and 4. Principals revised interview questions for new hires based on the Framework expectations.
Professional Learning Communities	Monthly	Principals attended these meetings with other principals clustered in the same geographical area. The content of these sessions was driven by the principals' needs. Principals brought samples of classroom observation notes, conference forms, and completed Frameworks to discuss with other principals. Administrators also shared shortcuts and tips.
One-on-One Technical Support	By request	Principals received one-on-one support from a highly trained observer. The principal and the observer co-observe a lesson, and the observer provides support in using the Framework to document that lesson.

Teacher Training

Teacher Training	When	What
School-Based In-Service Sessions	Two 1.5-hour sessions in the fall	**Session 1 (August before school started):** The principal introduced the session to all teaching staff, while district staff conducted the rest of the in-service. Initial overview of the Danielson Framework and the levels of performance. **Session 2 (October/November):** District staff led the session, which went deeper into Domain 3 (Instruction). Teachers also watched a video lesson, collected evidence, and rated the lesson.

Appendix D:
Quantitative Data and Statistical Models

Classroom Observation Data

The study benefits from a two-level stratified selection plan. At the first level, schools were randomly selected for participation in the Excellence in Teaching Pilot in the 2008–09 school year (N=43 schools). In the second year, 2009–10, the pilot schools included the initial treatment schools and an additional 58 schools (N=101 schools). At the school level, teachers were randomly selected from teachers in the pilot school who were eligible for formal evaluation. In 2008–09, the only eligible teachers were non-tenured teachers (typically in their first three years in the district) and tenured teachers with a low 2007–08 performance evaluation rating. In 2009–10, all teachers were eligible for evaluation.

The data consist of two types of observations: joint and solo. The reliability analysis hinges on a unique study design. To understand if principals were rating practice reliably, principals and external observers saw the same lesson at the same time but rated that lesson independently. We call these observations joint observations. When a principal or an external observer observed a classroom without the other present, we call these solo observations. We used ratings from principal solo observations to conduct the validity analysis. We used ratings from external observer solo observations to compare ratings in scheduled and unscheduled observations.

TABLE A3

Breakdown of joint and solo observations by year

Observation Type	Year 1	Year 2
Joint	277	222
Solo	n/a	2,930 (principal) 404 (external observer)

Models for the Reliability Analysis

We conducted two types of reliability analyses. First, we used hierarchical modeling to understand inter-rater reliability shown in Figure 3 and Table 4. Second, we used the many-faceted Rasch measurement analysis to understand differences in principal severity as shown in Figures 4-6. Here we provide more technical information on the reliability analysis.

Hierarchical Modeling

For our inter-rater reliability analyses, we used two-level hierarchical logit models, with information about the rating at Level 1 and information about the teacher, principal, and lesson at Level 2. All three of our models used binary outcomes based on the classroom observation rating, isolating different parts of the rating scale.

- **Low End of the Scale:** The model compares the likelihood of getting an Unsatisfactory rating to getting a Basic/Proficient/Distinguished rating. This model focuses on differences between principal and observer ratings at the low end of the ratings scale. The outcome equaled 1 if the rating was Basic/Proficient/Distinguished.

- **Middle of the Scale:** The model compares the likelihood of getting a Proficient/Distinguished rating to getting an Unsatisfactory/Basic rating. This model focuses on differences between principal and observer ratings in the middle of the ratings scale, which is where most of the ratings are. The outcome equaled 1 if the rating was Proficient or Distinguished.

- **High End of the Scale:** The model compares the likelihood of getting an Unsatisfactory/Basic/Proficient rating to getting a Distinguished rating. This model focuses on differences between principal and observer ratings at the high end of the ratings scale. The outcome variable equaled 1 if the rating was Distinguished.

The purpose of using these three models was to investigate the possibility that principals and observers were using the Framework ratings inconsistently. We do this in two ways: a) to check for main rater effects, and b) to check for component-level rater effects. In all models, ratings are nested within observations, allowing for the direct comparison of principal and observer ratings of the same lesson.

Differences in principals and observers at different parts of the rating scale. By main rater effect, we simply mean were principals rating in a different way than observers. In each of the models, there was an indicator variable that equaled 1 if the rater was a principal and equaled zero if the rater was an observer. If the coefficient associated with the rater variable is significantly different than zero, that means that knowing that the rater is a principal tell us something about what the teacher's rating will be. That is, without knowing anything else about the quality of the lesson, we can already predict the teacher's rating. In other words, principals and observers are consistently rating practice in different, predictable ways. The equation used to determine if there was an overall, or main, rater effect was the following:

Level 1 Model

$\text{Rating}_{ij} = \beta_{1j} (\text{Component 2a}) + \beta_{2j} (\text{Component 2b}) + \beta_{3j} (\text{Component 2c}) + \beta_{4j} (\text{Component 2d}) + \beta_{5j} (\text{Component 2e}) + \beta_{6j} (\text{Component 3a}) + \beta_{7j} (\text{Component 3b}) + \beta_{8j} (\text{Component 3c}) + \beta_{9j} (\text{Component 3d}) + \beta_{10j} (\text{Component 3e}) + \beta_{11j} (\text{Observation Round 1}) + \beta_{12j} (\text{Administrator}) + \varepsilon_{ij}$

Level 2 Model

$\beta_{pk} = \gamma_{p0}$, for p=1 to 11

$\beta_{12} = \gamma_{120} + \gamma_{12k}$ (vector of teacher characteristics)

The vector of teacher characteristics at Level 2—for both the main effects and the component-level effects—could include prior evaluation rating, tenure status, subject area, and grade level.

The odds ratios shown in Table A4 are presented in Chapter 3 in Figure 3 and support the findings on inter-rater reliability. Overall, principals and external observers used the low and middle parts of the scale consistently, as indicated by odds ratios not being significantly different from one. When it comes to high-level practice, principals are more likely to call it Distinguished when external observers call it Proficient, as indicated by the odds ratio being significantly above one (odds ratio = 6.18).

TABLE A4

Odds ratios from main rater effects logit models (N=9,920 ratings from 496 observations)

Variable	Low End of the Scale	Middle of the Scale	High End of the Scale	
			Level 1 Only	Level 2
Administrator	.74	1.00	6.18***	1.50 (L1)
Excellent Evaluation				3.13***
Superior Evaluation				5.37***
Year 1				0.49***
Social Studies				1.98***
PK				1.87***
K–2				2.38***
3–5				2.46***
Multiple				2.40***
Tenured				0.71*

Note: Asterisks indicate a significant effect: *** p<.01, ** p<.05, *p<.10. For brevity's sake, Level 2 covariates are only shown if the effect was significant. The excluded group for each group of variables is prior evaluation: Satisfactory; subject area: ELA; grade level: 6–8; and tenure status: non-tenured.

Differences between principals and observers component-by-component. As with the overall main rater effects described above, we can look at each of the ten components of the Framework to see if there are certain components where principals and observers rate teaching practice differently. For example, across the board principals and observers can generally agree about low-level practice (as shown in Table A4 above), but there may be some components where there are differences (as shown in Table A5). Districts can use this information to provide principals with more support in rating teaching practice in specific areas. The equation used to determine if there were component-level rater effects was the following:

Level 1 Model

$\text{Rating}_{ij} = \beta_{1j} \text{(Component 2a)} + \beta_{2j} \text{(Component 2b)} + \beta_{3j} \text{(Component 2c)} + \beta_{4j} \text{(Component 2d)} + \beta_{5j} \text{(Component 2e)} + \beta_{6j} \text{(Component 3a)} + \beta_{7j} \text{(Component 3b)} + \beta_{8j} \text{(Component 3c)} + \beta_{9j} \text{(Component 3d)} + \beta_{10j} \text{(Component 3e)} + \beta_{11j} \text{(Observation Round 1)} + \beta_{12j} \text{(Component 2a* administrator)} + \beta_{13j} \text{(Component 2b* administrator)} + \beta_{14j} \text{(Component 2c* administrator)} + \beta_{15j} \text{(Component 2d* administrator)} + \beta_{16j} \text{(Component 2e* administrator)} + \beta_{17j} \text{(Component 3a* administrator)} + \beta18j \text{(Component 3b* administrator)} + \beta_{19j} \text{(Component 3c* administrator)} + \beta_{20j} \text{(Component 3d * administrator)} + \beta_{21j} \text{(Component 3e* administrator)} + \varepsilon_{ij}$

Level 2 Model

$\beta_{pk} = \gamma_{p0}$, for p=1 to 11

$\beta_{qk} = \gamma_{q0} + \gamma_{qk}$ (vector of teacher characteristics), for q=12 to 20

TABLE A5

Odds ratios from component rater effects logit models (N=9,920 ratings from 496 observations)

Variable	Low End of the Scale	Middle of the Scale		High End of the Scale
		Level 1 Only	Level 2	
2a*Administrator	4.38**	1.07		5.55***
2b*Administrator	0.28**	0.93		4.02***
2c*Administrator	0.98	0.98		5.70***
2d*Administrator	0.38	1.47***	1.11 (L1)	20.19***
Excellent Evaluation			3.67***	
Superior Evaluation			4.79***	
Middle Grades			0.63***	
2e*Administrator	0.53	0.39***	0.52 (L1)	6.82***
Excellent Evaluation			3.66***	
Superior Evaluation			4.79***	
Cohort 1			0.46**	
Middle Grades			0.64*	
Tenured			0.42***	
3a*Administrator	1.19	0.77*	-0.34 (L1)	5.10***
Excellent Evaluation			1.03***	
Superior Evaluation			1.13***	
3b*Administrator	1.20	1.22		6.70***
3c*Administrator	0.98	1.48 ***	1.00 (L1)	10.90***
Excellent Evaluation			3.33***	
Superior Evaluation			5.17***	
Middle Grades			0.62**	
3d*Administrator	0.20***	0.74**	0.55 (L1)	14.83***
Excellent Evaluation			3.03***	
Superior Evaluation			3.93***	
3e*Administrator	0.56	1.12		3.66***

Note: Asterisks indicate a significant effect: *** p<.01, ** p<.05, *p<.10. Level 2 covariates are only shown if the effect was significant and if the Level 2 covariates explained the variation in Level 1. The excluded group for each group of variables is prior evaluation: Satisfactory; grade level: primary grades; and tenure status: non-tenured.

The Level 1 intercept is suppressed in all models. Doing this allows us to compare the component coefficients and component-rater interaction coefficients absolutely, rather than to an arbitrary excluded component. In all models, the component variables are uncentered, while the other variables are grand mean centered.

As discussed in the main text, when there are significant differences in the way that principals and external observers rate teaching practice (using the middle of the scale), many of these differences can be explained by the teachers' prior evaluation rating. For example, looking at the middle of the rating scale, principals sometimes rated teaching practice as Basic when observers rated it as Proficient. You can see this by looking at the table for the interaction between Component 3D and the administrator (coefficient = -.30 and is significantly below zero). However, when we control for teacher characteristics at Level 2, the effect is no longer significant.

It is worth noting that the size of the component-level rater effects at the low end and middle of the scale are much smaller than at the high end of the scale, supporting our emphasis on principal-observer discrepancies in ratings at the high end of the scale. Also compared to other characteristics, the effect of the teacher's prior evaluation rating is quite large, which suggests that the way principals rated teachers in the past is strongly related to how they rated teaching practice using the Danielson Framework and explains much of the difference between principal and observer ratings.

Many-Facet Rasch Measurement (MFRM) Analysis

A major component of this study is to determine if the Danielson Framework can be used reliably. Rather than using a simple Rasch model, which would not take into account the fact that there are many different raters or judges, we applied the MFRM method. MRFM extends the Rasch model to include additional facets. The MFRM analysis allowed us to investigate influences on teacher ratings in and among eight facets: teacher, component, rater (includes the three observers and each individual principal), rater type (observer or principal), cohort, observation year, subject area, and grade level. The model calculates the probability that a teacher will get a particular rating taking into consideration these categories, or facets, including rater severity. The model also provides us with a measure of rater severity for each of the individual observers and principals.

The data used in this analysis are 12,965 ratings from observations of 321 teachers in the joint observation sample across the two years of the pilot. The individual teacher measures of teaching ability generated in this analysis combine all Framework component ratings—from the observer and the principal across two years—for an individual teacher. The individual teacher measures are highly reliable (reliability=.93, separation=3.60). Teacher measures were created by aggregating the principal and observer Framework ratings for an individual teacher, which means that on average we had about forty ratings of these teachers. Separation indicates the ratio of signal to noise, which means that the instrument has almost four times as much signal as noise. In other words, the Framework ratings combine to produce reliable measures of overall teacher ability.

Another important findings is that it makes sense to treat each of the Framework components as distinct aspects of teaching (reliability=.98, separation=7.11). In this case, reliability is a measure of how well we can separate each of the components from each other, and the reliability of the Framework components is high (i.e., close to 1).

Models for the Validity Analysis

In Chicago, all teachers in grades 4–8 English language arts and/or mathematics all have value-added indicators. The Value Added Research Center at the University of Wisconsin developed classroom-, teacher-, and school-level value-added measures for CPS. These are the measures that we use in our analysis. These measures are based on student growth on the state test in Illinois (the ISAT). The models make adjustments for daily attendance, as well as student mobility. They also control for student demographics and prior achievement. The measures are standardized in order to make comparisons across grade levels. This means that a teacher whose students show average growth has a measure of zero. A teacher whose students show above average growth (1 standard deviation about average) has a measure of 1. A teacher whose students show below average growth (1 standard deviation below average) has a measure of -1. The measures for teachers in this sample run between -3.29 and 4.39 for reading and between -3.93 and 5.31 for math, though the measures cluster around zero.

Figure A6 shows the distribution of value-added measures for teachers in the pilot. Across the district,

value-added measures are fairly normally distributed, which is represented by the purple line in the graphs. The bars denote the number of teachers with a particular value-added measure who are in the analytic sample. We used a simple model to determine the relationship between the CPS value-added measures and the classroom observation ratings. This model was applied for each of the ten Framework components for both reading and math (a total of 20 models). We regressed the teacher's rating on each component (the intercept is suppressed, and there are dummy variables for each of the four possible ratings) on the teacher's value-added measure.

Validity Model

$$\text{Value-added measure}_{ij} = \beta_{1j} (\text{Unsatisfactory}) + \beta_{2j} (\text{Basic}) + \beta_{3j} (\text{Proficient}) + \beta_{4j} (\text{Distinguished}) + \varepsilon_{ij}$$

After running the regressions, we tested to see if the ratings explained a significant portion of the variation in the value-added measures (an omnibus F-test). We also tested to see if each of the coefficients in the model were different from each other. The coefficients are shown in Table A7.

Pilot teachers cluster near the middle of the value-added distribution

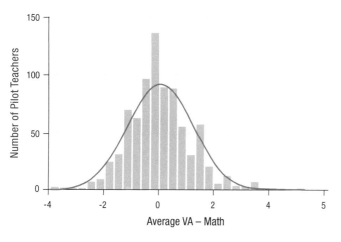

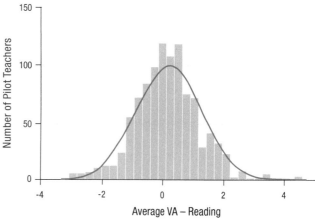

There is a significant relationship between observation ratings and value-added measures

Reading (N=795 observations of 417 teachers)					
Framework Component	Unsatisfactory	Basic	Proficient	Distinguished	Omnibus F-statistic
2a	-0.041	-0.162	0.226	0.264	5.33***
2b	-0.470	-0.086	0.186	0.411	6.60***
2c	-0.212	-0.083	0.170	0.364	4.67***
2d	-0.158	-0.04	0.175	0.326	2.94**
2e	-0.353	-0.026	0.180	0.430	4.99***
3a	-0.376	-0.054	0.191	0.305	4.13***
3b	-0.352	0.142	0.145	0.320	2.40*
3c	-0.111	-0.052	0.190	0.323	3.75**
3d	-0.338	0.005	0.239	0.391	5.39***
3e	-0.397	-0.087	0.201	0.429	6.87***

Mathematics (N=653 observations of 340 teachers)					
Framework Component	Unsatisfactory	Basic	Proficient	Distinguished	Omnibus F-statistic
2a	-0.030	-0.237	0.042	0.327	4.73***
2b	-0.552	-0.301	0.083	0.368	6.83***
2c	-0.105	-0.196	0.000	0.434	7.00***
2d	-0.359	-0.351	0.068	0.436	9.83***
2e	-0.165	-0.221	0.07	0.450	5.98***
3a	-0.639	-0.141	-0.011	0.370	6.60***
3b	-0.597	-0.043	0.085	0.299	3.09**
3c	-0.422	-0.160	0.062	0.335	4.10***
3d	-0.424	-0.076	0.08	0.424	4.48***
3e	-0.281	-0.104	-0.006	0.522	5.90***

Note: The table shows each of the ten components of teaching practice for which principals assigned ratings. The numbers in the rating columns are the average value-added measure for the teachers who received that rating in that component. For example in Component 3e, teachers with an Unsatisfactory rating had an average value-added measure of -0.397, which is more than one-third of a standard deviation below a teacher whose students achieved average student growth. The average teacher who received a Basic in 3e had a -0.087 value-added measure, Proficient had 0.201, and Distinguished had 0.429. In reading, for all components except 2a, the average value-added measure increases across the rating categories. The consistent correlation between the value-added measure and the classroom observation measure suggests that the Framework ratings are a valid measure of teacher practice.

Appendix E:
Qualitative Data and Analytic Methods

Year 1 Data and Analysis

Data in Year 1 consisted of 39 principal interviews and 25 teacher interviews. Principals and teachers were interviewed using a semi-structured interview protocol and were asked questions about: a) the professional development they and their teachers received; b) their perceptions of the Framework; c) their implementation of the evaluation system; d) the pre- and post-conferences they had with their teachers; and e) their perception of school change that had resulted (or could result) from implementing the Framework.

Interviews were transcribed verbatim and codes were generated using a combination inductive and deductive approach. Deductively, a set of initial codes were created to mirror the semi-structured interview protocol. Multiple researchers used these draft themes to code the same interviews. This was undertaken both to test inter-coder reliability and to inductively generate additional codes for themes that emerged in the data that were not captured by the draft codes. The team of researchers compared the coded text and identified and clarified areas of disagreement in the coding of the shared interviews. The inductively generated codes were integrated into the final coding scheme. Coding was undertaken using Atlas .ti, which is a qualitative analysis software.

Each of the transcribed principal and teacher interviews were coded using the tested coding scheme. Summary reports were run on each code such that all quotations assigned to each code were put together in a report. From these reports, descriptive summaries were created for each code. These descriptive summaries were combined and integrated where cross-code themes emerged. The purpose of these analytical summaries was to provide rich descriptions of principal and teacher insights, quantifying and grouping respondents wherever possible.

A second step was taken in order to better understand the clustering of attitudes evident in the coded text. For each code, principals and teachers were grouped into subsets. For instance, a grouping of "mostly positive," "mixed," "mostly negative" was used to summarize principals' attitudes toward the Framework. These subgroups were determined using the data, identifying subgroups that adequately represented the natural conceptual clustering within the data. These subgroup codes were then entered into a summary matrix for each principal and teacher to look for themes and patterns across codes.

An additional set of analyses were performed to measure principal engagement. Using the summary matrix for each principal, principals were grouped based on their responses on several questions that asked about the extent to which they implemented the evaluation system and their perceptions of and attitudes toward evaluation of teachers in general. In particular, the typology process aimed to provide information to CPS leaders about the extent to which principals in the evaluation pilot were engaging in the process, and the sophistication of these leaders to conduct teacher evaluation at a deep level.

A second round of coding was undertaken to identify additional themes that emerged within broader coding areas. This subset coding was applied to portions of the transcription that focused on the Framework, conferences, and implementation. The primary purpose of this subset coding was to expand our knowledge of important themes for the Year 2 data collection and analysis plan for 2009–10.

A final set of textual analyses were undertaken to explore the evidence data provided by principals and external observers. The primary purpose of this analysis was comparative. Evidence from the observation of the same teacher was analyzed for the principal and the external observer. This analysis focused on components that were identified as problematic, such as 3d (Assessment) and 2e (Physical Space). By comparing two observers' description of the same instructional practice, we hope to be able to better understand the reasons for the systematic differences in rating. At the time this report was written, these textual analyses were in the preliminary stages.

Year 2 Data and Analysis

Case Study Analysis

We collected data across 2009–10 in eight case study schools. The data collected included:

1. Principal interviews at three time points

2. Assistant principal interviews at one time point

3. Focus groups with teachers

4. Observation of 3–5 teachers as they engaged in the observation process (pre-conference to observation to post-conference to teacher interview)

Interviews and focus groups were transcribed verbatim, and codes were generated using a combination inductive and deductive approach. Deductively, a set of initial codes was created to mirror the semi-structured interview protocol. Multiple researchers used these draft themes to code the same interviews. This was undertaken both to test inter-coder reliability and to inductively generate additional codes for themes that emerged in the data that were not captured by the draft codes. The team of researchers compared the coded text and identified and clarified areas of disagreement in the coding of the shared interviews. The inductively generated codes were integrated into the final coding scheme.

Each of the transcribed principal and teacher interviews were coded using the tested coding scheme. Summary reports were run on each code such that all quotations assigned to each code were put together in a report. From these reports, descriptive summaries were created for each code. These descriptive summaries were combined and integrated where cross-code themes emerged. The purpose of these analytical summaries was to provide rich descriptions of principal and teacher insights, quantifying and grouping respondents wherever possible.

The observation data were analyzed in several ways. First, these observation series were coded to better understand the emergence of the Framework components in conversations between principals and teachers about instruction. A coding scheme was created with each component represented, as well as codes for general reference to the Framework. This was used to quantify the extent to which different components appeared in discussions in the conferences.

Second, observation series data were analyzed for evidence of the influence of relational elements on the conversations between principals and teachers. Early findings suggested the importance of the trust between principals and teachers as a foundation to have critical conversations about instructional practice. Coding was undertaken of observation data using a set of codes to capture relational influences. These codes were then analytically summarized.

Finally, analyses were undertaken to consider the depth of questioning in conferences. A rubric was developed, loosely based on the Danielson Questioning component. This rubric was then applied to textual excerpts from each case study principal. These analyses were used to assess the overall depth of questioning across case study principals, as well as to characterize individual principals.

Principal Engagement Survey Analysis

A bank of items was constructed around the five different themes we used to qualitatively categorize administrators in the first year of the study: attitudes toward the Danielson Framework, conferences, estimates of teacher buy-in to the system, and assessment of the influence of the evaluation system on instructional practice. A set of questions was created around each of these concepts, using the responses of principals in interviews in the first-year study as a guide for the topics and response categories.

We used Rasch modeling to construct measures around each of the concepts. Applying Rasch to each of the clusters of items led to the creation of four measures: 1) administrator evaluation attitudes, 2) administrator attitudes toward conferences, 3) administrator estimates of teacher buy-in, and 4) administrator estimates of changes in instructional practice resulting from participation in the evaluation pilot.

Endnotes

Chapter 1

1 The New Teacher Project (2007).

2 The New Teacher Project (2007).

3 McLaughlin (1990); Searfross and Enz (1996).

4 Haefele (1993).

5 Haefele (1993); McLaughlin (1990).

6 Darling-Hammond (1996); Eisner (1992); Van Sciver (1990); Wise et al. (1984); The New Teacher Project (2007); Small Newspaper Group (2005).

7 U.S. Department of Education (2009).

8 Performance Evaluation Reform Act, Illinois Public Act 096-0861.

9 The New Teacher Project (2007).

10 The Chicago New Teacher Center began providing induction support for most new teachers in the school district in 2009–10. Their instructional coaches use a modified version of the Danielson Framework to support teacher development. The Chicago Teacher Advancement Program, a pay-for-performance model in high-needs schools that focuses on developing teacher leaders through providing increased professional opportunities, also uses a modified Danielson Framework as the classroom observation tool.

11 The observers were three practitioners who were on loan to the CPS central office from their schools for the purposes of this study. The three external observers have specialized knowledge: one is a special education teacher with National Board certification, another is bilingual, and the third has both teaching and administrative experience. The observers received intensive ongoing training around using the Danielson Framework, including an initial three-day training, follow-up support focused on specific components, and practice observations in actual classrooms. All training of observers was in a small group setting.

Chapter 2

12 The Value Added Research Center (VARC) at the University of Wisconsin developed classroom-, teacher-, and school-level value-added measures for the Chicago Public Schools. These are the measures that we use in our analysis. These measures are based on student growth on the state test in Illinois (the ISAT). The models make adjustments for daily attendance, as well as for student mobility. They also control for student demographics and prior achievement. For more documentation on the CPS value-added measures, see http://research.cps.k12.il.us/cps/accountweb/Research/ValueAdded/.

13 The pattern is a little less consistent in reading in Creating an Environment of Respect and Rapport (Component 2a) and in math in Creating an Environment of Respect and Rapport, Managing Classroom Procedures, and Organizing Physical Space (Components 2a, 2c, and 2e, respectively). For these components, the average value-added measures for Unsatisfactory teachers and Basic teachers are similar. One potential explanation for this is the fact that principals assigned few Unsatisfactory ratings, so the number of teachers in that category is small.

14 Tyler, Taylor, Kane, and Wooten (2010).

15 Baker et al. (2010).

Chapter 4

16 Costa and Garmston (2002).

Chapter 5

17 Known as the vitality curve, Jack Welch's widely used but also widely criticized performance evaluation philosophy relies on a ranking of employees. The top 20 percent are rewarded with promotions and raises, the middle 70 percent are productive but not leaders, and the bottom 10 percent should be removed. See http://guides.wsj.com/management/recruiting-hiring-and-firing/should-i-rank-my-employees/.

18 This district uses different criteria for tenured and pre-tenured teachers. We use the less stringent criteria, those for pre-tenured teachers. It should also be noted that this district also accounts for Domains 1 and 4 in their evaluation. To be consistent with the rest of this report, we use only Domains 2 and 3.

19 These joint observations allowed us to conduct the reliability work.

20 The training detailed here describes the support provided for Cohort 1 principals in their first year of implementation. Training was scaled back for Cohort 2 principals. These principals received two days in the summer and two refresher days during the school year.

21 In Year 2, teacher leaders from each school were invited to attend a two-hour train-the-trainer session. The district intended for these leaders to redeliver the training in their schools; however, according to central office staff, this did not occur in many schools.

22 While assistant principals can conduct one of the two formal classroom observations, the principal assigns the teacher's final evaluation rating.

Conclusion

23 Lortie (2002).

About the Authors

Lauren Sartain

Lauren Sartain is a research analyst at the University of Chicago Consortium on School Research, as well as an associate researcher at Chapin Hall at the University of Chicago. Her research interests include teacher quality, school reform, and human capital. Her current research involves looking at trends in post-secondary and employment outcomes of Chicago high school students. Lauren has a B.A. from the University of Texas at Austin and a M.P.P. from the Irving B. Harris School of Public Policy at the University of Chicago, where she is currently a doctoral student.

Sara Ray Stoelinga

Sara Ray Stoelinga is senior director at the University of Chicago Urban Education Institute, as well as an associate clinical professor on the Committee on Education. Stoelinga leads research projects focused on teacher quality, teaches within the University of Chicago Urban Teacher Education Program, and teaches and advises undergraduate and graduate students at the University of Chicago. Stoelinga received her B.A. and Ph.D. in sociology from the University of Chicago.

Eric Brown

Eric Brown is a research analyst at the University of Chicago Consortium on School Research. He is currently working on a three-year evaluation of a digital media learning initiative for high school-aged teens. In addition to the Excellence in Teaching Pilot work, Eric's past projects at CCSR include providing research and data support to school leadership teams in a small network of schools and an examination of the transition between middle school and high school. Eric received his B.A. in Liberal Arts/Social Sciences from the City University of New York (CUNY) and an A.M. in Social Service Administration from the University of Chicago.

This report reflects the interpretation of the authors. Although CCSR's Steering Committee provided technical advice and reviewed earlier versions, no formal endorsement by these individuals, organizations, or the full Consortium should be assumed.

This report was produced by CCSR's publications and communications staff.

Editing by Ann Lindner
Graphic Design by Jeff Hall Design
Photos by David Schalliol

11-11/.75M/jh.design

Consortium on Chicago School Research

Directors

Paul D. Goren
Lewis-Sebring Director
Consortium on Chicago
School Research

Elaine M. Allensworth
*Senior Director and
Chief Research Officer*
Consortium on Chicago
School Research

Melissa Roderick
*Hermon Dunlap Smith
Professor*
School of Social Service
Administration
University of Chicago

Penny Bender Sebring
Founding Director
Consortium on Chicago
School Research

Steering Committee

Ruanda Garth McCullough
Co-Chair
Loyola University, Chicago

Matthew Stagner
Co-Chair
Chapin Hall
Center for Children

INSTITUTIONAL MEMBERS

Clarice Berry
Chicago Principals and
Administrators Association

Karen Lewis
Chicago Teachers Union

Connie J. Wise
Illinois State Board
of Education

INDIVIDUAL MEMBERS

Veronica Anderson
Communications Consultant

Andrew Broy
Illinois Network of
Charter Schools

Amie Greer
Vaughn Occupational
High School-CPS

Reyna Hernandez
Illinois State Board
of Education

Raquel Farmer-Hinton
University of Wisconsin,
Milwaukee

Timothy Knowles
Urban Education Institute

Dennis Lacewell
Urban Prep Charter Academy
for Young Men

Lila Leff
Umoja Student Development
Corporation

Peter Martinez
University of Illinois
at Chicago

Gregory Michie
Concordia University
of Chicago

Lisa Scruggs
Jenner and Block

Brian Spittle
DePaul University

Luis R. Soria
Ellen Mitchell
Elementary School

Kathleen St. Louis
Project Exploration

Amy Treadwell
Chicago New Teacher Center

Arie J. van der Ploeg
American Institutes
for Research

Josie Yanguas
Illinois Resource Center

Kim Zalent
Business and
Professional People
for the Public Interest

Our Mission

The Consortium on Chicago School Research (CCSR) at the University of Chicago conducts research of high technical quality that can inform and assess policy and practice in the Chicago Public Schools. We seek to expand communication among researchers, policymakers, and practitioners as we support the search for solutions to the problems of school reform. CCSR encourages the use of research in policy action and improvement of practice, but does not argue for particular policies or programs. Rather, we help to build capacity for school reform by identifying what matters for student success and school improvement, creating critical indicators to chart progress, and conducting theory-driven evaluation to identify how programs and policies are working.

CPSIA information can be obtained
at www.ICGtesting.com
Printed in the USA
LVHW071054230723
753216LV00002B/31